When the Devil Laughed:

A Memoir

by Phyllis Redman

ISBN: 978-1-953596-09-3 (paperback)

ISBN: 978-1-953596-10-9 (e-book)

Library of Congress Cataloging-in-publication data
When the Devil Laughed: A Memoir, Redman, Phyllis

LOCN: 2021902494

Cover Design by Eric Labacz

The Publishing Portal
Los Angeles, California

Printed in the United States Of America

To Kathy Sheeder Bonanno

Telling your story is an important tool for healing.

–Alexandria Ocasio-Cortez

Contents

Foreword

We never know where our friends will come from, who will stay, and who will go, and certainly when I met Phyllis at Helpline Center in Lansdale, PA in 1970, I had no idea we would become lifelong friends.

There are so many things I remember from the beginning days of our friendship: meeting her parents, Leon and Sylvia, over a brunch of lox and bagels at her townhouse at the Brookside Manor apartments. The Jiffy cornbread she always made, as well as Italian salad dressing. Her lack of inhibitions when she danced and wishing I could be more like her and her boys, so small when we first met. Phyllis taught me to knit - I wonder what happened to that bright green sweater... And our trip during the summer of 1976 to West Virginia, in her VW van with David, Robert, and baby Jason and all our most prized possessions.

That summer was unlike any other - living in a verdant West Virginia holler, at times baking in a wood-burner oven, using an outhouse... or worse. I have many fine memories from that summer, but returning to Philly in September brought the darkest times, when Phyllis's ex took her to court for custody of David and Robert. Losing your children is bad enough, but the underhanded way it happened was enough to drive anyone a little mad. I believe it did drive Phyllis a little mad. She loved those boys. Fortunately, she had Jason, whose presence and need of his mother, along with the support she eventually drew from Sylvia, pulled her through that long, darkest of times.

Most of all I remember her unconditional love. Phyllis is one of the most open, emotionally generous persons I've ever had the good fortune to know. She's also one of the least judgmental I count among my friends. She may have been hard on herself, but she's never hard on others. Friends like

Phyllis Redman

Phyllis, who offer what is close to unconditional love, are friends you should hold onto.

At that old, red brick building on South Broad Street in Lansdale, torn down to become a parking lot the last time I looked, so many friendships began and grew, and so many changes occurred that affected the course of lives, maybe especially Phyllis's life.

Here is the story, Phyllis's story.

—Barbara DeMarco-Barrett

Corona del Mar, CA, January 2021

Prologue

I hadn't expected that dismantling my mother's world would be so difficult. I was sad, but her death, at almost ninety-three, was neither tragic nor unexpected. She'd been ready to go for a long time. "Why am I still here?" She'd ask when I came for my daily visit to the hospice center where she spent the last three months of her life.

"You need help, mom," I'd reply. "You can't live alone anymore." She'd been in her own apartment all this time, feisty and independent as always. She cooked, cleaned, did her laundry and only after I took her car keys (against mighty protests) did she allow me to take her shopping.

"No, no. Why am I still alive?" She'd give me a funny little half smile.

Although our relationship had been decidedly less than smooth for most of my life, the last few years had brought a healing between us. Her cold, critical mothering had left a lot of scars, leaving a hunger that had led to many a calamitous decision. But in these years she'd softened; I'd forgiven. I thought I was prepared to lose her, but as I emptied her cabinets and drawers, sorrow weighed as heavily on my shoulders as the ankle-length mink coat I slipped into while going through the coat closet. The one I had loved to wrap up in naked when I was a child. There too was the gorgeous mint green satin gown she wore to my brother's Bar Mitzvah and the brightly colored beaded bag with its red and green and yellow painstakingly sewn flowers, a timeless and exquisite work of art... except for the torn strands at the top, dangling like teardrops from the metal clasp. That was Mom, a damaged beauty.

My mother had an eye for beautiful things, but for people it was more the eye of the critic, the kind that pummels a child's self-esteem relentlessly. "Here, let me do it. You're not doing it right." "Wear a padded bra, you're too flat-chested. You want the boys to like you, don't you?" And over and over, "Why can't you be like everybody else?"

The kind of criticism that caused so much pain that I withdrew almost totally from family life. I closed my bedroom door and longed for the happy, supportive mother of my dreams. The one I was determined I would be.

Now I watched my three sons and their wives pick through the jewelry and china, choosing a few items to keep in the family. There wasn't a lot anyone wanted. My youngest son, though, surprised me, tearfully claiming his grandmother's framed needlepoint collection. She'd loved him but hadn't always been kind to him. But she was family, to a young man who didn't have much of that. His relationship with his brothers was... well, I'm getting ahead of myself here.

There was one item I discovered in the back of the big hall closet that shocked me. The paper was yellow and flimsy, all two-thousand-some pages of the transcript from the custody hearing that changed my life forever. The one I lost. Why in the world had she kept it?

I stood there all these years later, holding the huge, crinkled wad of paper, grieving the loss of my mother, remembering how my own children had, in a sense, lost theirs. Almost forty years ago. Some experiences never lose their wallop. Some pain lingers forever. I could still see that courtroom, hear the lawyers' voices, the judge's questions, feel the sweat of fear, the breathlessness of despair.

Without thinking, I rushed to the trash room a few feet from the front door and dumped the mound of tissue-like paper into the incinerator as if it were on fire. As if what was in it weren't permanently burned into my soul.

I'm sure there are things I've forgotten, but mostly I remember only too well. I remember conversations and accusations and the pitch of lawyers' voices. I remember crowds outside the courthouse door and the grooves in the stone steps leading into the courtrooms, visible before my lowered eyes. I remember the years of darkness before I began to heal, and then live again. It took a long time.

Phyllis Redman

Chapter 1

Stepping Out of the Box

It was April, 1971. A Tuesday evening. Above the roof of the Lansdale YMCA, the lavender sky threatened a spring storm. Nervous and excited, I stood in the parking lot, the wind pressing my short skirt against my thighs, carefully styled hair tossed like the salad I'd just made for dinner. I was twenty-four years old and about to take the first completely independent step of my entire life, one hardly preordained for nice Jewish girls from upper middle class, suburban families. With no clue where it might lead, I stopped before entering the building to breathe in the warm, spicy scent of the approaching rain, and to gather the courage to go in.

All my life I'd tried hard to play the role I was told led to happiness, first in high school trying to at least look like everyone else with my soft Papagallo loafers and mandatory round-necked, Villager shirts. I got good grades and joined so many committees that I rarely left school before 5 pm. I looked like I belonged, but I never felt it. I was different, concerned with politics and poverty and all kinds of things my friends didn't find interesting or important. "You can't worry about the whole world," they told me. But I did.

As the suburban hausfrau I still played that game, in pursuit of the perfect outfit, the *House and Garden* home, the ideal family. I was still trying to be what I'd been told I should be. I had everything I was supposed to want, or so my husband, Paul, said repeatedly, and based on what I'd always heard, he was right. But I was miserable. I tried to be satisfied, I really did, but one man, two kids, and a house full of Danish modern furniture just wasn't enough. I felt locked inside an attractive, wall-to-wall carpeted box. There was so much world out there, so much that needed doing. At that time, the country was well into the Vietnam "military action" and the terror of my boys growing up only to die one day in some awful war on the other side of the globe was growing in my gut. I wanted to do something to change the way things were, to help create a peaceful world in which my boys would be safe. I wanted people to talk with about the things that mattered to me, and Paul had little interest in anything outside work, sex and dinner.

Helpline Center, where I was headed, was one of many grass-roots referral centers sprouting up all over the country in the early seventies. It was housed in two rooms at the rear of the Y's upper level, next to the Lansdale Bowling Alley on Main Street. Anyone with a problem could call for the name of one of the professional doctors, lawyers or social workers who donated their services, or simply for someone to talk to. Potential volunteers for the phone lines were interviewed on Tuesday nights, I was told when I called. "Come in any Tuesday, around seven," the young man said, and there I was. I had no idea what to expect.

I entered a dimly lit hallway, where a boy, maybe seventeen, sat on an old school desk, his long hair falling to his shoulders in tangled waves. "Hi, I'm Jerry," he smiled broadly and extended his hand.

"I'm Phyllis. I called last week about volunteering." I offered my hand in return.

"Sure, sure. I remember. It was me you spoke to. Meeting's right over there." He pointed to a doorway halfway down the hall. "See you there in a few."

This room was also dimly lit, with candles flickering on a narrow table along one colorless cinderblock wall. A dozen or so young people, all with long hair and faded blue jeans, sat in small groups talking. One man, clearly older than the others, sat on another small desk, feet propped on the seat and a clipboard full of papers in one hand, talking to a beautiful girl with long blond hair, dark eyes and pale full lips. His brown hair fell just below his chin, where a bushy mustache ended. He looked up and met my eyes briefly.

Each of the five newcomers was interviewed by a different person, from a script of possible scenarios that could come up on a call: a boy contemplating suicide, a fifteen-year-old girl who just found out she was pregnant, a drug problem, a lonely teenager. Mike, the older man, took my interview.

I began as we were instructed. "Hello, Helpline Center. This is Phyllis. How can I help you?"

"I want to go to bed with you," Mike said, his face expressionless, except for the candlelight reflected in his eyes.

Wow, did they really get calls like this? His eyes held mine steadily this time.

"Well, uh, maybe you need to find someone closer." I was at a loss, so I said the first thing that came to mind. Everyone laughed.

"No," he replied softly, "there's no one close. No one I can even talk to."

I handled the call just right, it seemed, easing myself into the sympathetic listener the lonely caller needed. By the end of the interview I felt completely at ease. Was Mike testing me, asking a question like that? How much of a proper suburbanite was I, in my trendy purple minidress?

Would I be comfortable with the kinds of issues I might face? Or was there something more at play here? I ignored the slight increase in my heart rate. It was just my imagination, I was sure.

Mike was co-director with Tony, the chief of the Juvenile Division of the Lansdale police department, who was mentioned in the Sunday Inquirer article that led me to Helpline Center. After the interviews, Mike took us on a short tour of the phone room and the tiny office, explaining how the phone bank worked, length and frequency of shifts, things you could and couldn't say on a call, what the training looked like. We were shown a list of people who were available for referrals... doctors, lawyers, shrinks... who volunteered their services.

When I left two hours later, the rain had come and gone, leaving puddles twinkling like good news under the Y's bright spotlights. Bursting with excitement I entered my townhouse eager to share what I'd experienced. My husband looked up from the TV, eyebrows raised. "Well, did you get this craziness out of your system?"

That stopped me cold. "What do you mean, 'craziness?' Is it crazy to want to do something that might make life better for our sons? Is it crazy to want to be involved with what's happening in the world?" I was furious, not just at his disregard for what mattered to me, but for what was happening in the world we lived in.

"A bunch of long-haired freaks aren't going to make the world any different." And with that, he turned back to the television. I didn't say another word.

Thursday afternoon I got the call to begin training sessions the following Monday night. Excited and defiant, I told Paul, "You'll have to watch the kids and get them to bed. I'll be training the next three Mondays and then I'll have one or two shifts a week. I'm doing this, Paul.

"It would be great if you'd come over and see what it's about." I threw my sweater over my shoulders and paused before opening the door to go out for a walk, hoping for some reaction, for some small sign he might want to share his wife's excitement. He didn't even turn around.

Training was interesting. Along with the particulars of the job, there was conversation about politics, the war in Vietnam, what it would take to create the kind of world where it was okay to simply be who you were. Although not entirely sure who that was, I was beginning to acknowledge how much I was not the person I'd been trying so hard, for so long, to be. The first thing I did was stop straightening my hair and sleeping on rollers the size of soup cans. Who I really was, was someone with wild, frizzy hair. Out went the razors. And the bras.

"What the hell have you done to your hair?" Paul asked dourly, twirling one finger around a curly strand at my temple. "It looks like a half-used Brillo pad. When I also stopped shaving everything I usually shaved, he was disgusted. And not wearing bras? He became obsessed with the thought of my nipples being visible. "Let me see," he checked every time I went out.

"They're just breasts, Paul. They feed babies. Not everyone is thinking about sex all the time." I wasn't actually so sure about that, but it wasn't what was on my mind.

Chapter 2

Endings and Beginnings

Mike and I became friends quickly. At first he called me once in a while, with tidbits of news like schedule changes, or to tell me about a new member, but soon we were talking every day, on his work breaks or in the middle of the night, whispering softly so as not to wake anyone. Somehow, miraculously, we didn't. I stubbornly refused to consider that anything more than friendship was happening. I was so hungry for this kind of conversation.

Mike had four children, a wife, a full-time job setting up displays in supermarkets, two little brothers in the Big Brother program, a beloved Irish setter named Rusty and his work at Helpline. He was out there doing what I'd only dreamed about. I was awed. I envied his wife, sharing life with someone so giving, so involved. I pictured her with long, swishy hair and bell-bottom jeans... an image wildly off-base, as I was to discover.

Helpline became the center of my world, the friends I made there my family: Mike, a girl named Cindy, Barb, the beautiful, dark-eyed girl I'd seen with Mike that first night. They all lived in a world very different from the one I'd known, a world far less stringent in its definition of what was or was not acceptable. Mini dress or bell-bottoms, frizzy hair or straight, old or young, all okay. Brand new townhouse or cabin in the woods, brick and plywood bookshelves or rich teakwood, all good. Feeling like a psychic girdle I'd been crammed into forever had been loosened, I dove into this new environment happily. I felt at home, for the first time in my life. I was no longer the oddball who cared too much and showed her feelings too openly. How many times had I heard, "Everyone doesn't need to know how you feel?" But I'd never figured out how to hide.

But the easier I breathed there, the more stifling life with Paul became. Again I tried to open my heart to him. "Please come and share this with me," I implored. "Just give it a chance. Shit, Paul, it's what I'm all about. Don't say you love me if you're not interested in who I am."

Eventually Paul did make a brief visit to Helpline with me, nervous and uncomfortable in the presence of those long-haired, "hippie freaks," but by the time he did, the divide was too great. It didn't matter to me anymore if he reluctantly accepted my absences or grudgingly came over, leaving as quickly as possible without a word to anyone. It just wasn't enough. For the first time in my life I was among people who looked at the world the way I did, who respected me just the way I was, and I wanted that. My hunger was too big and too deep, and I didn't want to beg for understanding from anyone. I was getting it.

Paul would have had to be someone, well, not Paul. I truly didn't want anyone to feel they had to be something they weren't, any more than I wanted to. I tried to get him to see that he would be happier with a partner who shared his values and desires. In my need and naivety, it all made perfect sense. To me. It felt right when I'd felt wrong forever. I could still hear my mother's voice, "Can't you do anything right, Phyllis? Why do you always have to be different?" I wanted to be like everyone else, but I didn't know how to be anything but what I was being. Now I found myself in a world that allowed me to feel comfortable in my own skin. Nothing was getting in the way of that!

One afternoon, while Robert was napping and David was at kindergarten, Mike called. "Do you have any idea how lonely I am? I mean for someone to share my heart with, someone who gets what my life is really about?"

What? I almost dropped the phone that was wedged between my chin and shoulder, as I stuffed wads of wet clothes into the dryer. Did I understand? "What about your wife?"

"My old lady thinks I'm crazy, that I've got no business giving so much time to other people's kids when I've got four at home. She wants nothing to do with Helpline... or anything else I'm into. I can't do life like she wants... just our little insulated family. There's a world out there that needs fixing. That *is* for my kids."

I was nearly in tears. "How could she not love someone who gives so much to the world?"

And with that, the walls came tumbling down. The loneliness, the resentment, the longing for a kindred spirit, all the need burst through the pretense of friendship we'd worked so hard to maintain. The hunger consumed me. "I love you," I whispered, the words falling from my lips like sugar from a tipped over canister.

"I love you too," he whispered back.

When I wasn't at Helpline with Mike, I dreamt about him. Pushing Robert on the swings, reading bedtime stories, I longed to share those moments with him, to share every moment of our lives. I wanted my boys to have a father like him. I didn't have one iota of reservation, when normally I questioned every decision I made. There was no decision here. He was my soulmate; of that I had no doubt.

On the infrequent occasions we could get together outside Helpline, we grabbed a meal and even went to the movies once. We did all sorts of silly, romantic things, like finishing each other's sentences, and weeping together, fingers entwined and vibrating with longing, when everyone else was laughing at a gawky teenage boy having his first sexual experience in the movie *Summer of '42*. I longed for Mike, but he wanted to preserve what he called the "purity" of what we felt until we were both free, and he actually meant it. I was the kind of full that threatened to burst the pores of my fingertips and ribcage. Surely this was what those nineteenth century poets were feeling when they wrote those mushy poems we snickered at in high school.

I'd wanted out of my marriage for a long time; I just never thought I'd have the courage to leave. How did you tell someone you shared a life with, "Sorry, I'm done, go make your own life and leave me alone?" That was what I felt... just go, please, I hate this life we have, I can't breathe. You don't care what matters to me, you don't even try to understand me. I've spent six years trying to get you to hear me, and you haven't, and I'm fucking done. I wanted to scream it.

Instead I placated him. "You deserve better," I told him. "I'm just not cut out for this." Want this too, I thought, hate me, if that's what it will take to get you to leave. But what I said was, "It's all my fault. I'm a lousy wife and mother."

Paul agreed. And actually, after listening to him, and my mother, for six years, I believed it too. I had no perspective on myself. Maybe I was crazy. But right then, I didn't care. Right then, I just wanted to be whatever I was in a world that seemed to find that person acceptable. So I'd be a crazy woman in a world of crazy people. Maybe... but as far as I was concerned, this was the sanest world I'd ever experienced.

I gave it all careful consideration. Did I want to risk being alone if by some unimaginable chance Mike and I didn't make it? Could I handle being a single parent? I didn't want to have any regrets. I hated that this would hurt my children, and even Paul. I didn't want to hurt anyone. But I wanted out.

The divorce was an ugly business. Paul would not leave the house and, a lawyer I contacted from Helpline's list told me, I couldn't force him to because his name was on the lease. I could go, but I had nowhere to take two little boys and I just had to get away. So I left alone and stayed at the old house that Helpline had just leased to open a walk-in center, a big three-story stone building that was once the home of some well-to-do businessman. I claimed a space on the top level, sleeping on a mattress on the floor with pictures of my kids around the room, feeling exuberantly and sadly free.

Having married at nineteen, this was the first time in my adult life that I was alone. A part of me wanted to walk away from all of it... Paul and being a parent. I was a mother by the time I was twenty and never had a time that was all mine. Even as a child I'd spent a considerable amount of energy trying to fix the dysfunction in my family that of course I couldn't possibly fix.

Not carefree at all. The excitement of being accountable to no one for what I did with my time, or where I was, buzzed through me like little electric currents zapping all my pleasure points. For a few days. But I realized quickly that I didn't want to leave my children. I missed their weight in my lap, their little hands in mine, our bedtime rituals. I missed their beautiful faces, their innocence and trust and funny little idiosyncrasies. Maybe I wasn't a great mom, but I loved my kids. All I'd ever wanted was to be a good mother and have a happy family... unlike the one I grew up in.

When I returned to the townhouse a week later and announced that I was not giving up the children, Paul went crazy, slamming me into the washing machine and punching me over and over, with David standing behind him, pulling his shirt and crying for him to stop. Hearing my screams, a neighbor called the police.

"You should file charges, ma'am," the officer told me seriously, scribbling something into a small notebook in his hand. But I couldn't do it. I felt so guilty. If I filed charges, he'd have a record. I was taking everything from him. This was my fault.

"I just want him to go," I told the officer. "Just make him leave."

Paul promised he'd be gone by the end of the month. I was too tired to argue.

But the end of the month came and went, and he remained. I called the police station and asked for the officer who'd come to my home. He said it was too late for him to do anything about the matter. I should have filed charges at the time. Two more months went by in a tense limbo. I slept on the couch downstairs. The lawyer told me what to do and what not to do, including staying away from Helpline, and Mike, until Paul left the house. That was hard. I was afraid all the time.

Phyllis Redman

Chapter 3

A New Normal

After almost three months, Paul found an apartment and was finally packed and ready to go. I stayed away until late on the day he left, hanging out at Helpline with David and Robert. Rob was not yet two and didn't understand what was happening. But David, at five, got it. I explained to him with the usual daddy-and-mommy-can't-live-together-anymore-but-we-both-still-love-you storyline, that he'd still see his father regularly, but worry clouded his dark brown eyes and sadness curved his straight little back. I was so sorry for them to lose an intact family, but I knew only too well that growing up surrounded by dissension and anger didn't go a long way toward creating a happy childhood... or a healthy adult. Of that I had no doubt at all.

When I returned home, the sight of the half empty living room stopped me in my tracks. The couch was gone as was the wall unit that held the TV, which was now sitting, unplugged, in the middle of the floor. From the bedroom Paul had taken exactly half the teakwood set that I'd paid for with the savings bonds my grandfather gave to each of his grandchildren every year on their birthdays. I loved that exotic wood, its straight, clean Danish lines. We hadn't talked about what he'd take. We hadn't talked at all. I just wanted him to leave. Still, I was surprised. And angry. I'd been so preoccupied anticipating the relief of Paul's absence that I hadn't for a moment thought about this. The house felt empty and cold.

I also hadn't considered loneliness. I'd never lived by myself, and although solitude was not uncomfortable, this was different. I wasn't really alone, my children were with me, but without another adult, solitude somehow shifted into a deep sense of aloneness. More than the lack of help with daily life, the weight of responsibility lay heavily on my shoulders. I was baking this parenthood cake from scratch, with nothing from my childhood to guide me. I certainly didn't want to raise my boys in the unpleasant way I was brought up and I had no experience of anything else. Doing it alone only amplified that weight. I wanted so much to do it well.

I wasn't part of any world I could learn from either. My new friends were young and only Mike had children. My neighbors and old friends who did have kids still lived in the box I was leaving behind and now kept their distance. Nor did I desire contact. They were perfectly good parents, but there was something about them that made me feel less than, somehow inferior, just as Paul and my mother did. Theirs was a world where I always felt alone, with no one to share so much that was important to me. Now I was a hippie freak, something that world neither understood, nor wanted in their lives.

I was making it all up as I went along, trying to believe that I knew what I was doing. Looking back, I think I actually did, in some respects at least. I talked to my kids and treated them with respect. I applauded their artwork, their efforts at school, how well they made their beds. I said, "I love you" and hugged them a lot. I hoped this was good parenting. I knew these were things I hadn't experienced in my childhood, behavior I'd longed for. But I felt there were other important things that I was unaware of. A single parent, one with no family support has only herself to rely on. And what, I wondered, did I really know?

My friend Cindy was my savior. She was born to be with children. She was endlessly patient, good-humored, playful and warm. Her full figure and twinkly eyes invited a child to climb into her lap and snuggle, twining little fingers through her long, silky brown hair. Nothing alarmed her and she never got tired of playing. Me? I had no idea what play looked like. That was another thing missing from my childhood; there'd been little lightheartedness or fun. I was almost as much in Cindy's care as my boys.

Gradually life relaxed into its new normal. The townhouse was often full of people in tie-dye and jeans, always jeans. We were young, pumped up with the faith that changing the world was possible and that we were the ones to do it. We were on a mission. We'd tame the beast of human nature with our smiles and kindness and determination, with a limitless tolerance that would bring peace to the world. Corny as it sounds, we believed this. I believed it. Flower children indeed, young, naive and hopeful. Such were the times.

David and Robert were swept up into our garden, happy with all the attention and company. They were, in fact, thriving. I'd never experienced a world where children were so much a part of the world around them. There was nothing we did that excluded them. They were good boys, sweet and easy, and I discovered that I liked being a mother. My unhappiness, which I'd thought included being a parent, had nothing to do with them at all. My real life, the one I'd longed for forever, had begun.

Only one thing marred this happiness. Mike, who had moved out of his house into a small apartment nearby, began to withdraw into some private place that excluded me. Stunned, I tried to talk to him, to get through the barriers he suddenly built around his heart, but little by little he became someone I didn't know at all. I had no idea what happened. Reeling and heartbroken, I focused on my children and my new life, leaning heavily on Cindy, Barb and another new friend named Lisa for support. They wouldn't allow me to talk about Mike and did a pretty good job distracting me, although the sadness was always there, quietly resting in my heart. But not for a moment did I regret the decision I'd made.

Soon after welcoming in the new year, when Paul and I had been apart for several months, I got a letter from my friend Caroline, who lived down the hall when we were freshmen at Miami University in Ohio. "Frankie and I are coming east," she wrote. "Can we stay with you for a while on our way through Pennsylvania?" Her husband, Frank, was Paul's fraternity brother. They were the ones who introduced me to my future husband. Of course they could stay with me.

When they arrived a few weeks later I was happy to see them, although more than a little shocked to discover they'd found Jesus while tripping on mescaline in the Oregon forests. Their "little while" turned into three months, during which time they pounded everyone I knew with their proselytizing. However, Caroline was the most endearing human being I'd ever met, and we all knew this was an act of love to her. The tolerance I'd found and so loved, the universal respect was extended even for this. Their visit was, all in all, wonderful. I loved having the company, loved sharing my new life with Caroline. Paul, however, refused to see his old fraternity brother. "Oh well," Caroline said with a shrug, "some of us just get lost."

In the early spring they left for upstate Pennsylvania, where they planned to spend the summer with friends on a large farm near Scranton. "Why don't you bring the kids up for a while, Phlea?" Caroline asked, using my old college nickname. "It's a big old place and there'll be some interesting people there. Good folks. The boys will love it."

"Maybe," I answered. "I'll think about it." It sounded like fun, fresh air, a garden, company. I was ready for something new.

I missed them right away, but it was good to be alone with time to sort through all that had happened in the past months.

Phyllis Redman

Chapter 4

My First Commune

When school ended the third week in June, we packed up the little dark-green Austin America my father bought me when Paul left and headed north toward Scranton. Through the lush green countryside of Northeastern Pennsylvania we gazed out the car windows at old farmhouses splashed over the rolling hills like a tipped over Monopoly board. White fencing wove across fields of grain and corn, marking off huge square patches of land where horses swatted their tails lazily and cattle grazed with slow deliberation. The open sky above us sat like a wide blue and white bonnet of heaven.

The house, a big, white clapboard throwback to a hundred years ago, sat at the top of a long, steep driveway. In a huge garden off to one side of the house I saw Caroline bent over a young tomato plant, a large straw hat shielding her freckled face from the hot sun. There were two other people working in the garden, and a man in denim overalls coming through the front door, a round compost container in hand. Caroline looked up and waved as we pulled onto a gravel parking area.

"You made it! Welcome. I'm so glad you came," she called out, smiling broadly.

We hugged and were introduced to the seven other people there for the summer, in what was considered an experiment in communal living. There were two teachers, a nurse, a Vietnam vet, a couple of hippies who were friends of the owner (a doctor who would be coming up on weekends) and a young woman from Sweden who met Caroline and Frank in Oregon. Several were born-again Christians like they were. David and Robert, who held tightly to my leg, shyly peeking around my thigh at all these unfamiliar faces, were the only children, and were welcomed with great enthusiasm.

Surprisingly, I took to the garden immediately, even though I'd never before grown more than a few annuals outside our townhouse. I loved the pungent scent of the tomatoes, the peacefulness of sitting in the dirt, sun hot on my back, pulling up the weeds that threatened to choke the little plants. I checked each day for the tiny, perfectly-shaped peppers, poking out where the day before they were only small white flowers. The squash vines were just beginning to curl along the ground and sported a few bright yellow flowers.

Many afternoons were whiled away sitting on the wraparound front porch, the sun warm on our feet, sometimes in silence and sometimes in long, serious conversations. Like the ones at Helpline, they were soaked with idealism and hope and determination. I mostly listened, taking in new ideas, humbled by the worldliness of people who, I felt, knew so much more than I. Often the focus was on spirituality, a concept I'd never given much thought. Everything in me resisted the idea of organized religion, but this was a new slant on the word, a simple one focused on people simply being kind and respectful toward one another. Well, that I could relate to! "C'mon people, smile on your brother, everybody get together, try and love one another right now," as Jesse Colin Young crooned. How simple an idea, yet so difficult for people to do. Why was that? Wasn't that what religious teachings were all about anyway? Or supposed to be.

Once a week two or three of us took the kids and went into a little nearby town for provisions, returning with a dozen or so cartons filled with bread, cereal, and pounds of the brown rice that was served every night, a sticky grain that took me years to make peace with. Milk and produce were bought more frequently at a small working farm just down the road. We'd also stop at the town library, where David loaded up on the chapter books he loved and sometimes an art store for crayons, pens, and paper for drawing. David was an avid reader, like me, and both my kids loved to draw. Their pictures were tacked up all over the house.

In the evenings, most of us gathered in the living room, sometimes attempting to watch an old television hooked up to a crooked, wire-hanger antenna, more often singing or telling stories.

Robert, no longer shy, would snuggle up to one of us until he fell asleep; David would sprawl on the floor, reading or drawing, all the while listening intently to the conversation going on around him.

Several weeks into our visit it started to rain, a relentless downpour that continued for almost a week. Power went out and we couldn't use the phone or the toilets. There was talk among the born-agains about another biblical-style flood and a spooky excitement permeated the house. The kids were nervous, but for the rest of us it became something of a cosmic adventure. Even having to use an old outhouse about two hundred yards from the back door was part of the mystique, although David and Robert were grossed out and Rob's potty training hit a snag for a while.

We learned eventually, when the rain finally stopped and we could get into town again, that this had been a newsworthy event, that power was out for miles around, and there'd been considerable damage to many of the farms, roads and local bridges. We were without power for almost two weeks, using oil lamps, candles and flashlights, and moving perishables to a cool root cellar probably not used in half a century.

When things finally returned to normal, we were all well aware and appreciative of the blessings of modern technology... and at the same time we'd enjoyed the simplicity and closeness we'd experienced weathering the storm together. This was how I always believed a family should be.

Chapter 5

Through The Barn Floor

In mid-July, Paul came up to Scranton to see the kids. Although Frank was his fraternity brother, and his friend, Paul refused an invitation to join us on the porch for some iced tea and conversation, and nervously gathered David and Robert and wandered off with them. An hour later, Frank came running into the living room and grabbed my hand.

"C'mon, Phyl, quickly," he muttered, pulling me hard to the door and out toward the barn. "There's been an accident."

Panic washed over me instantly. The kids! But they were with Paul.

But Paul and Robert were nowhere to be seen, and David was lying in an odd position on a pile of broken bricks, stone and glass on the lower level of the barn.

"He fell through the floor... up there," Frank said softly, pointing to a gaping hole in the upper level floor, at least ten feet above us. "We've been working on repairing it. The kids knew it was off limits. I don't know where Paul and Robert are. I haven't seen them."

Oh my God, oh my God! I ran to my son, who was moaning and crying, in a strange high-pitched voice, "Is this really? Where am I? Am I dead? I can't see, mommy. Is this really?"

"Do something. Help him," I sobbed. There was no word for the scope of my fear, which slithered and wrapped around my bones squeezing the breath from me.

"We've called an ambulance, they're on their way," Tom, the Vietnam vet said, grabbing my shoulder firmly. "You have to stay calm for him. Get it under control."

Tom was a medic in Nam, he'd seen worse. But I hadn't. This was my child! My beautiful six-year-old son, with his thick dark hair and big brown eyes and the straightest little back I'd ever seen. With his serious demeanor and sweet kindness. I was wild with fear. But I managed, somehow, to calm myself... outwardly at least... enough to kneel by David and take his hand. I knew I couldn't move him, so I stroked his hair and told him over and over that he would be alright, he'd be fine, praying that would be true. Not ever had I been so frightened.

As I climbed into the back of the ambulance and sat down beside my son, Caroline took my hand and whispered, "We'll be praying. Jesus will take care of your baby."

I looked at her briefly, panic and tears clouding my vision.

A piece of David's skull was pushed in and was pressing on the optic nerve. Somehow nothing else was broken. He was rushed to surgery where they shaved one side of his head and removed the broken fragment of bone. After the surgery, I sat beside him, praying and loving him for hours... I had no idea how long... begging for him to be alright, until he awakened sometime late that night.

At some point, Paul arrived at the hospital. "Where the hell did you go?" I growled at him, all my fear woven tightly like the inside of a baseball that I pitched at him full speed. "Why did you leave him there alone and not tell anybody? He's only six-years-old. What were you thinking?" I wanted to rip him into tiny pieces I could blow into oblivion, the years of silently absorbing his criticism and condescension packed tightly behind my panic.

"I took Robert to get ice cream. David didn't want to go. You have no business being in a place like this or it wouldn't have happened."

His face was pale, eyes frightened and dark. He was going to blame me for this? Was he kidding? He wouldn't even speak to anyone, just because they had long hair, never told us he was leaving, and David was in the barn. I was too angry to speak.

"I'm taking Rob to the motel. He doesn't need to be here."

Yeah, run away, I thought, but I didn't say anything. I really didn't want him around.

I stayed with David until morning, when the doctors assured me at last that he would be okay. His vision had returned, and he was lucid. I kissed my six-year-old's forehead. "I'm going back to the farm to shower and change and then I'll be back, sweetie. You're going to be fine. Tom will be here with you."

He nodded. "Come back soon, mommy," he whispered.

One of the teachers took me back. A few minutes into the drive I noticed the clouds had formed a cross above us. I pointed it out and watched as it remained directly above our car the entire fifty-minute trip. When I told Caroline later, she smiled. Told you He'd look out for your baby."

I was, at that moment, exhausted and beyond astonishment, aware only that there was something that could be called miraculous going on. Miraculous and significant... but that is for another story.

When David was released from the hospital a few days later, I just wanted to go home, back to Lansdale and familiarity. Caroline begged me to stay, with the support of the people there around me, but I was worn out. David would be better off at home, with his friends around, where it was safe. Guilty again. If I hadn't been up there, it wouldn't have happened.

Chapter 6

The Next Step

By the middle of August David was back to his normal self, running with the local kid crew of neighborhood youngsters. I, however, was not. As much as I didn't want to instill my fearfulness in him, it was all I could do not to hover over him like a bee at its favorite clump of goldenrod. When Paul planned a week at the shore with the kids, I was relieved. Surely he'd be watchful on familiar terrain. They'd have fun and I could relax. But a vague uneasiness fell over me the moment they were gone. I just didn't trust Paul.

Days after the boys returned from vacation I received a petition for custody that Paul filed, basing it on my negligence in taking David and Robert into a dangerous environment, failing, of course, to mention that they were in his care at the time of the accident. My instincts had proven accurate. I fled sobbing to my father, who called his attorney immediately.

The petition was withdrawn a week later. I didn't ask who did what or how. I didn't care.

The next time Paul came to see the kids, my father was waiting. He stayed until they returned and then followed Paul outside. When he came back in he was laughing so hard he had to sit down. "I told him if he ever did that again I'd hire worse than a lawyer. He just took off running to his car."

On New Year's Eve, 1972, my father suffered a massive coronary. My daddy, the one person in the world who always had my back, who felt like real family, like someone who cared, was gone on January 6th. He was the one who came to babysit, whose voice I'd hear from the next room, every single visit, "Once upon a time there were three bears..." and then his booming laugh. The one who shooed me away while first David, and then Robert slept for hours on his chest. The one who made them giggle and made me feel safe and not so alone. I was stunned and heartbroken.

And then, one by one, my closest friends left Pennsylvania. Barb went to Goddard College in Vermont, and Cindy and several others went out west. Mike was long gone, not to another physical place, but to some inner world that excluded me and most of the others who loved him. Friends said he was drugging hard and not the man I remembered.

My world became small and lonely. I began thinking about a new life somewhere else, one where Paul couldn't hurt me, where there'd be family for my children. The idea took root and slowly blossomed into a plan. Caroline and Frank had settled in Arizona and extended a standing invitation for us to join them there. Cindy's letters from Colorado were full of exciting news of counter-culture activities and alternative lifestyles. Please come she wrote at the end of every letter.

The thought of taking off scared and excited me. I'd never done a thing on my own before. But I didn't see anything where I was that might bring me the life I wanted. It was, I decided, time for the next step.

Phyllis Redman

Chapter 7

Wild Hopes

By early August, almost a year since we'd seen Caroline and Frank, I had it all together and was ready to go. I'd sold all I could and either given away or stored what was left in a friend's garage. On a hot summer morning David, Robert and I stood quietly on the dusty parquet floor of the empty living room, knowing it was no longer our home. Pale, ghostly shadows eyed us solemnly from the walls where my new age posters had hung since Paul moved out. Robert's four-year-old hand rested trustingly in mine, but David stood aside, eyes cloudy like the heavy summer sky outside. At eight, he understood that his world was plunging into some vast and mysterious... and unwanted... unknown.

"Do we have to go, mom? I don't want to," he said softly.

"Hey Dave, it's gonna be okay," I reassured him. "I know it's hard. Just trust me." I leaned over and looked into his big chocolate eyes and held him close for a moment, speaking

47

with a conviction I only partially felt, a wild hope that soared across my inner landscape, careening awkwardly around the corners of my own doubt.

David remained quiet, unconvinced, looking for all the world like an abandoned polar bear adrift on a lost fragment of ice. I couldn't expect my son to welcome this, I knew that. Or to understand why we were leaving. I certainly had my own fears. Part of me wanted at that moment to just undo this decision, to bring back our beds and everything else I'd sold and stay put in the world I knew. But Paul was a threat always hovering vaguely around my shoulders, and the world I knew wasn't offering what I wanted, which more than anything else was a safe place for my children to grow up in and people who cared about and paid attention to them. In other words, a family.

I'd heard stories about what was happening around the country... communal living and political involvement, living in harmony with the natural environment. A world where you didn't have to pretend anything to be respected. Like at Helpline, only on a bigger scale. I wanted that for my children, and I wanted it for myself. After most of a lifetime feeling like a total misfit, this sounded like a world where I could feel at home, with people who had the same values and hopes that I had. Only years later did I understand that I was driven as much by loneliness as by ideals.

Outside, my friend Joan, who lived across the wide lawn beyond our front door, waited with her son and daughter to say goodbye. Josh and Heather were my children's closest friends. They looked like bright, blonde flowers lighting up the gray afternoon. My heart ached to disrupt this little family our children had created. I didn't know then that the three of them would be on their way to Minnesota the following summer, where Joan's fiancé would be relocated.

Joan's eyes were closed, arms folded across her chest. When she heard me approach, she looked up and smiled, a small, sad twist that only touched the corners of her mouth. "Are you sure about this, Phyllis? You don't have to go through with it." Joan had made it clear that she thought it was a bad idea.

"Ah, but I do, Joanie." Aside from pursuing a dream, everything we owned was either gone or packed tightly into the little Honda Civic I bought with the small inheritance I'd gotten from my father. I so missed his stifling bear hugs, and the wet, sloppy kisses I hated when I was younger. What I wouldn't have given for one of those hugs right then! My mother, brother and sister somehow didn't feel like family, at least not the family I longed for, who spent time with my boys and gathered for loud, chaotic, table-laden festivities on the holidays. That was the most painful time not to have family to offer my kids. They barely knew their relatives. My mom rarely saw them since my father died and wasn't particularly nice when she did. My sister lived in New York and neither came home nor stayed in touch, and my brother was away at school. Neither showed the slightest interest in David or Robert. Or me. God I wanted a family. "It's a done deal, Joan. You know I have to do this. I'm not happy here."

"But you could be," she began, and stopped. "I hope you find what you need."

The six of us lingered, the sky pressing down as if its weight would hold us there, safe in the familiar, if unsatisfying, parameters of the life we knew. It was really hard to say goodbye. There were tears and promises to stay in touch that I suspected wouldn't last long. David and Heather, who were the mommy and daddy to the local kid crew, clung to each other.

49

"Promise me you'll write, David. Promise," Heather pleaded.

"Yeah, I will. You promise too," David answered sadly.

Oh my God, what was I doing? A fine drizzle began to fall, the tears I refused to shed. Fear and excitement, hope and sadness mixed a hot stew in the cauldron of my belly as we headed to meet Cindy, who'd come back from Colorado to accompany us on our journey, and my friend Misha, with his tangle of long blond hair and dirty PF Flyers, who wanted to check out the western scene too, where so many of our friends had found their brave, new world. I was happy to have company for whatever was coming next.

Chapter 8

On The Road

Our destination was Caroline and Frank's home in Tucson. The journey across the country was staggering in its magnitude, its novelty, its logistical complexity. I'd never done anything remotely like this in my life! Two young and restless boys were stuffed into the back seat of a small car, laughing, bickering, making up road games, complaining. I heard "Mommy, I'm bored" more times than I ever want to hear those words again. Potty stops, meals, lodging, all things to be considered. At one point we traveled an extra hour, retracing our steps to find the sneaker David threw out the car window to see how long it would remain visible as we sped away at seventy miles an hour. It took him a long time to get up the courage to tell me.

We were a two-car caravan of hope and intention, rolling across the varied landscapes of America by day, stopping at motels or KOA campgrounds at night, where we met friendly travelers from all over the country. Heady with the scent of adventure and freedom, I breathed it in deeply as each mile carried me further from all I'd ever known.

Our fourth day out we rolled across the Texas Panhandle, a thin, flat plate of earth below a vast, cloudless bowl of deep blue sky. I'd never seen so much space. East coast crowds, traffic and small blips of sky spotted between buildings and above rooftops were what was familiar to me. Here I was, a tiny ladybug creeping across an endless boulder balanced on the edge of the world. This enormous sense of smallness was, for some reason, very comforting. I felt held and safe, with the vague awareness of something bigger and more powerful than anything I was familiar with.

Cindy and Robert were riding with Misha in his old Saab station wagon, rattling along behind the little Honda that Cindy called "the toy." The few vehicles we saw invariably contained a local cowboy type, tee shirt sleeve rolled to the shoulder around the square of his cigarette pack, short hair stirring slightly in the open window of his pickup truck. All these Marlboro men, but no other young, suburban mothers carting their two young children into the unknown.

No one knew our itinerary. In fact, only my closest friends even knew we were leaving. I mailed letters to my mother and Paul on our way out of town. Not the way I would have chosen to do it, but Paul had already tried to take the boys from me, and my father was no longer here to protect me. My fear of Paul was always with me, fueled no doubt by my chronic self-doubt.

My mother approved of nothing I did anyway and had subjected me since David was born to endless criticism about my parenting. Fold the diapers this way, not that; hold him higher to burp; don't feed him apricots, give him beets! Oh, a little sugar won't hurt them, she'd say as she piled boxes of candied cereals, that I didn't allow, onto the kitchen counter.

I didn't want to hear their arguments, their discouragement, to explain and defend myself again and again. I knew this wasn't really fair to Paul, but when had he been fair to me? I needed to go. I wanted to go. I was tired of trying to be fair, of trying, however ineptly, to be good. There was a better world for my kids to grow up in, one where I could find some peace. Or so I hoped. Other than the people traveling with me, no one on earth knew where I was at that moment. Like the red-winged hawks that soared above us, I was free in a way I'd never been before. The future, somewhere down the long, blank highway before me, beckoned from the horizon, with all its mystery and possibility. What would it look like when I got there?

Chapter 9

Land Of Enchantment

"There" began when we crossed into the "Land of Enchantment," as the bright yellow New Mexico license plates claim. Tucumcari was a tiny alley lined with a half dozen rough wood buildings sitting with bored ambivalence along the interstate: a tavern, a post office, a gas station and, oddly, a Chinese restaurant, that months later would be significant in shaping the rest of my life. A few more unidentifiable structures lined the road and I wondered how such a jumble of bare wood and scrub qualified as a town. Only a few homes were visible as far as we could see, which was a considerable distance.

The view was dry and dusty and a dozen shades of brown. Even the low-lying mountains showed only the slightest bit of green amid the rich, velvety cocoa of the rounded hills, looking like crowds of dachshunds sitting at attention. Exotic and wildly liberating, little doors popped open in my internal landscape, revealing a longing for something I didn't recognize, something primal and ancient that suddenly felt vital to my existence.

The twentieth century slipped away, and I could almost hear the thud of buffalo galloping across the open plains, almost see the teepee villages and the dark-skinned Indian children running through the dry summer days, hear their laughter ripple across the wide expanses. What was the strange sense of connection I felt there?

"I'm hungry, mom," David asked, snapping me back to the present. He and Robert had been very quiet. Were they awed by this landscape too?

"Sure, Dave. We'll stop to eat at the next place we see."

"Yeah, well it looks like that'll be awhile. Rob's hungry too," he added, thinking, I knew, that I'd take this more seriously if the baby of the family needed to eat.

"Hey, Rob, how're you doing back there," I called over my shoulder.

"I'm hungry too. This place is lonely. Where are all the people?" he answered.

I promised him we'd get to a city before night, where there would be lots of people. Robert never liked to feel alone. He was the one who held my hand wherever we went, something that I wished would somehow last forever.

I saw that my sons weren't nearly as taken with this place as I was, not so receptive to the barren, unfamiliar terrain, the lack of human presence, the silence. What was bright and intoxicating to me was shadowy and foreboding to them.

We were hours from Albuquerque. There had to be somewhere to eat on this long, empty road, I thought.

We approached Albuquerque well past sunset. The city lay to the south, visible from miles away, like a mirror of a planetarium's sky. So many stars! So many lights after the long darkness. Rob was happy to see this panorama of civilization.

I stopped at the first motel we saw on the outskirts of town, next to a Denny's restaurant whose lights glowed yellow and red against the night sky. The kids clamored for dinner there, although it had only been a few hours since we ate an unappetizing lunch at a roadside diner we'd finally come to. I registered at the motel, one room for Misha and the boys, another for me and Cindy.

That was a great adventure for the kids, spending the night with Misha, just the menfolk, separately from me.

"Wash up guys and we'll get some dinner," I called as they ran to their own room.

Cindy raised her eyebrows. "Denny's?" She'd had enough grease for one day.

"Sorry, Cin. I can't stand another minute in that car. They're hungry, as much for something familiar as for food."

She nodded, dropped her backpack onto the nearest bed and headed to the adjoining room. Through the open door I heard her teasing the boys about their poor choice of dining places. David defended his position with customary seriousness, but Robert giggled. Greasy burgers were something he knew, and he adored Cindy.

After we ate, David and Robert plunked down for some TV time in their room. I was asleep almost before Cindy closed the door.

In the morning we packed the car and headed into downtown Albuquerque, a beautiful twentieth century American city, sunny and clean. The light in New Mexico glowed golden under the endless turquoise sky, a different quality altogether from that in the east. In those last days of August the air was balmy and dry and gently caressed my skin. People moved without hurry. Every muscle and molecule of my body responded to this place, so alien and yet so familiar. Had I been here before, in some other life, I wondered?

We strolled around the city for a few hours, looking in store windows at turquoise jewelry and tooled leather belts, handwoven baskets and colorful shirts sporting familiar Native designs. We ambled slowly through an Old West museum, alive with displays of cowboys and horses and Indian villages. Heading back to the car, we stopped at a health food store for some sandwiches and decent snack food and chatted with the young man at the register. He asked where we were from, where we were headed, why we were there.

"Oh, you'll want to see Santa Fe while you're in these parts," he told us enthusiastically. "It's just a ways north. Shouldn't get this close and not see Santa Fe."

I looked over at Misha and Cindy, who were basically tagging along on my adventure. We were in the flow... no schedules or watches, just vague plans that opened each morning like golden day lilies. Cindy nodded. Misha shrugged. I was aware that it wasn't that long until school began and that I wanted to be settled in time for David to attend the first day. I was not ready to relinquish public education or to ditch the system completely as some people I knew had, in favor of home schooling.

I was drawn to everything about this golden land, whose past seemed to echo in my soul. I remembered how much I loved the old cowboy shows of the 1950's, like Hopalong Cassidy, the Lone Ranger, Gene Autry and Roy Rogers. I was suddenly aware that I'd felt the same unidentifiable longing, watching those Hollywood cowboys gallop across the black and white plains that seemed so real to me then.

Chapter 10

Through The Rabbit Hole

A few miles south of Santa Fe the interstate became Cerrillos Road, a long, dark ribbon winding through acres of stubby piñon trees, speckled with fat round cones, all studded with tiny brown pine nuts. I found out later that the pine nuts only come out every seven years and we lucked into that seventh year. We spent one glorious afternoon picking them, our hands thickly coated with the gluey sap-like substance that holds the nuts. Past the piñon trees, one short strip mall boasted a McDonalds, a gas station and a few small shops. Across the plain a housing development rose against the horizon, where the split-level homes offered an odd mixture of contemporary style and ancient adobe.

Downtown Santa Fe took my breath away, only partially because it sits more than six thousand feet above sea level. From a distance it looked like a sunny watercolor, framed by the pale, sandy scrub of the plains, the dark green of Hyde

Park rising behind the pink adobe, with a turquoise canopy of sky above. Adobe was everywhere... homes, shops, government buildings, even a JC Penny.

In the center of the town the Plaza held court, a magnanimous queen dowager sharing her dazzling treasures with pride. Dozens of Native men and women, skin bronzed by the sun, sat cross-legged around the square, their crafts spread around them like booty salvaged from sunken Spanish galleons. Human works of art themselves with their beautiful, sculpted faces, adorned with feathers and beaded moccasins, they wove bright blankets and baskets made from long, yellow reeds. Their tiny hammers rang out tinkling melodies, molding silver into earrings and wide bracelets inlaid with turquoise and shiny black obsidian. Earth-toned pots with intricate Native designs, and fetish necklaces made of dozens of polished stones lay scattered around the blankets on which they sat.

I'd fallen through the rabbit hole, Southwest style! Despite the proximity of fast food restaurants and cheap department stores, I was no longer in twentieth-century America, but transported in the golden light into the place I was longing for in Tucumcari. I could not, at that moment, imagine anywhere I would rather be.

And Caroline and Frank were waiting for us.

We spent one night in the capital city and reluctantly headed southwest in the morning, toward Tucson. The change in altitude, the stunning beauty we were leaving behind, and the disorientation of a week on the road were all taking their toll. There was so much "new." I felt unsettled and listless. David and Robert squabbled irritably in the back seat and Cindy was silent.

By the time we got to Tucson we just wanted to stop. Caroline and Frank welcomed all five of us warmly, for which I was grateful, considering the invitation was just to me and my boys. I was surprised by their appearance. Frank's beard was gone, as was their long hair. Both his and Caroline's were cut short and neatly styled. She was wearing a pale, uninteresting shirtwaist dress and Frank was sporting pressed slacks and a light blue, button-down shirt. No more jeans, no tie-dye. I found out quickly that Frank was in the process of becoming a minister. Had it really been only a year since I saw them?

As much as I appreciated their warm welcome, my stomach ached with unease. September was only days away, which meant school. I was all over the place about where I wanted to be, standing with each foot in a different world entirely. On the one hand, I longed to go back to the "Land of Enchantment;" on the other, it would be nice to start over with friends who were settled and knew the lay of the land.

Caroline and Frank were sweet and attentive to the boys for two days while I slept or sat quietly, trying to decide my next step. Tucson did not appeal to me, although it was a pleasant enough city. But despite the sandy front yards and the cacti, it felt like going back to what I left behind: a modern city going about its business as usual. It didn't look familiar, but it felt it. Would any place have been as magical as Santa Fe? And I wanted magic. I wanted different.

On the third day, Caroline finally confronted me, with her sweet smile and soft voice. "Okay, Phlea, what's it gonna be? Should we start looking for an apartment for you and the kids? Are Cindy and Misha staying with you?"

No, Cindy and Misha were not staying with me. Not if I stayed there. Cindy wanted to return to Santa Fe and Misha was looking toward Colorado.

"Oh Caroline, I so appreciate the offer, and your hospitality," I said, almost as surprised as she by the words coming out of my mouth. "I think... I just fell in love with Santa Fe."

Caroline smiled, a little sadly. "Are you sure? We have such a nice community here, a small church, with a school. Lots of kids."

Church? Church school? Oh I don't think so, I thought to myself. If I hadn't been sure before, I was then. I hugged my old friend. I loved her. And she and Frank had turned a sharp right and gone completely Barry Goldwater, while my rebel Jewish soul was barreling headlong in the opposite direction entirely.

Two days later we were on the road again, driving back through the desert into the morning sun toward Santa Fe.

Chapter 11

The Invitation

The first thing I did upon arrival in Santa Fe was look for a newspaper. All I wanted at that moment was to find a place to call home. Misha hugged us each goodbye and turned the wheezing Saab back toward the interstate, north toward Colorado. David's eyes reflected clearly his reluctance to see yet another familiar face slip away. I felt for him, but my mind was elsewhere. Cindy put an arm around each of my children. "How about some lunch, fellas?"

I gave them each a peck on the cheek and went to a payphone on the busy corner, my fist full of coins.

I found a house right away, a tiny, one-story adobe on a small patch of sand on Fayette Street, in what was called the barrio. I had no idea what a barrio was, or that we would be virtually the only non-Hispanics in the area. I had no idea that

65

at dusk the Natives around the Plaza packed their pots and jewelry and blankets and returned to the outlying reservation. I was unaware that the relatively small number of white residents in the area lived well outside the city limits, in sprawling, pink dwellings that merited display in *Home and Garden* magazine. I was simply relieved to have somewhere to call home.

Fayette Street was a wide, flat avenue about five minutes from the Plaza. Most of Santa Fe proper was five minutes from the Plaza. Each house on the street had a small front area, which in the east would be a lawn, but here was either sand or hundreds of small, round stones. It didn't feel like a ghetto, but I learned shortly that "barrio" was the southwestern word for just that. I was actually charmed by those little houses and the sense of space that the vast sky and the distance between buildings created. I was not so charmed by the snarling German shepherds that flew to the edge of almost every property, fangs bared, when anyone walked by. So much for walking to the Plaza.

The house had a kitchen and four other rooms, each opening into the next. We spent the following days going to yard sales and flea markets, buying beds, a couple of dressers, a small, round white rug for the living room, a couch, a TV. There was no refrigerator, but I discovered that it was cool enough to preserve milk and butter, which I bought in small quantities and kept on a shady ledge outside the kitchen window.

I registered David at the nearby elementary school, which opened in a few days. The principal told me, with obvious concern, that he would be the only white child there. I thought, great, what an experience! Sharing cultural differences and learning Spanish maybe. It would be life-enriching. Words like "prejudice" and "trouble" didn't come to mind. Only later did I understand the extent of my naiveté, my very limited understanding of the larger world around me, having been cloistered in the suburbs most of my life.

Being the only white child in a barrio school, I came to find out, was not a good thing. Maybe being the only anyone anywhere, people being what they are, was never a good thing. David was a trouper; he never complained. It was months before I learned what he was experiencing. He was my good boy, eager as always to please, a serious child who always took on more responsibility than was asked of him, as I think first-born children tend to do. Just like I did, feeling always that it was up to me to hold my world together since no one else appeared to be up to the job. I tried my best to impress on David that I was there, in control, that he was safe and didn't have to figure things out. Or so I liked to think.

The health food store along the Plaza became our umbilical cord to the life of the city. While the residential population was almost entirely Hispanic, the surrounding area was inhabited by Native Americans, wealthy white artists and celebrities, and a growing number of counter-culture hippies, many part of a community called *La Hermandad de Cristo*, the *Brotherhood of Christ*.

Most of its members lived on a sprawling commune several miles outside town, but a dozen or so stayed in a roomy building, once some kind of business, a block from the Plaza. Every night they cooked an enormous amount of beans, rice, tortillas and vegetables and fed anyone who dropped in for a meal, or some company, sometimes twenty or thirty people at a time.

The members of *La Hermandad* were young. Both men and women alike had long hair... streaming silken tresses that made me think of shampoo commercials, clouds of frizz, bushels of thick, fly-away curls. All that hair just sang of youth and rebellion and freedom... freedom to be whatever you chose to be.

I took David and Robert there for dinner almost every night during our first weeks in town. Cindy had discovered a neighborhood tavern and immersed herself in the local culture, joining us only occasionally. At first the boys and I were quiet, sitting close together and observing the scene around us. There were often other children, depending on the night, and although my kids were shy at first, little by little they began to mingle. This journey had brought them into the kind of closeness I always wanted for them, the kind I never had with my sister and brother. No matter what, they had each other. "Together" made it easier to meet new people and face new situations. Together makes a lot of things easier.

One night a man named Jose walked in. I'd seen him before, but not like he was that night... staggering drunk and clearly enraged. He had a thick stick in one hand and a gun in the other. A young woman named Linda saw my face, reached over and whispered, "Don't be afraid. He gets like this sometimes." But I was afraid. Shaking in my boots terrified afraid. I pulled David and Robert closer to me, ready to shield them if necessary.

"Jose's wife died last year, from a drug overdose. He's a sweet man really, but now he goes on these binges, raging at the world," Linda told us. "He just doesn't know any other way to deal with his pain. But he won't hurt anyone."

I was not convinced. David and Robert both scrunched up against me. We watched in horror as Jose swung the stick and shattered the big, storefront window. "Why?" he roared. A half dozen men and a few women surrounded him, speaking gently. He swung again and then doubled over onto his knees, sobbing. They took the gun and held him until he was quiet, then led him into the eating area, where he sat cross-legged on the floor beside the long, low table until his emotions were spent. One young woman sat beside him silently, her open hand resting lightly on his balled fist.

I looked around. It was very quiet. I didn't understand how everyone was so calm. I was a wreck, and at the same time awed by what I'd just seen. And what I hadn't... mainly fear. There wasn't a sign of it anywhere. Was it because they knew Jose? Why had no one called the police? There was broken glass all over the place, but no one was hurt. No one, other than me, was visibly disturbed at all. What did they know that I didn't? Where did courage like that come from? We all said we wanted to live in a peaceful world. Well, this looked like walking your talk. Like real peace, love and understanding.

While Jose's meltdown had rattled me considerably, *La Hermandad* was my only connection to other people. The magic of Santa Fe was beginning to wear thin under the rub of daily living in a place where I knew almost no one, a place that was alien in every way. Although friendships were budding with a few of the women there, I only saw them at dinner for a couple of hours. I didn't know what to do with myself all day. Cindy had very quickly fallen in love with a young Mexican and moved in with him. She stopped by frequently, but the afternoons were long, the nights solitary. I missed her good humor, her fearlessness, her affection for and attention to my children. I missed her company. My fears were sprouting like weeds after rain, as were my doubts about what I was doing there and how to create the life I longed for.

What did a better life actually look like? Company? Other mothers with young children? A career? What could I do? I'd lived twenty-six years in a small, safe world that hadn't asked very much of me other than the most fundamental things: meals, a clean house, bedtime stories, hugs and kisses. I was a babe in the New Mexico woods and so much younger than I'd thought.

One day Cindy took Robert to the playground while David was at school. Alone in the little house on Fayette Street, alone with my fears and confusion, I had a total meltdown and did something I didn't often do. I prayed. I didn't really know who or what I was praying to, I just cried out from a place deep within that I was not familiar with. I felt lost and I needed help. I needed some kind of guidance.

The following night at *La Hermandad,* one of the members announced they were closing their doors for the next several weeks. The members were going on retreat at their property outside of town until a week after Thanksgiving. It was then the fourth week in October.

Leslie, one of the women I'd become friendly with, was sitting beside me. She'd been staying at the Brotherhood with her husband, Scott, and their two-year-old, Pahana. She was obviously familiar with Santa Fe and the members of the commune. A tall, lanky woman with silky blonde hair, Leslie reminded me of wild grass swaying in the dunes by the ocean. Her calm demeanor drew me like the sunlight enticed the jagged leaves of the big, potted aloe that sat in the newly repaired front window. Without a thought, I turned to her after the announcement and invited her and her family to stay with us while *La Hermandad* was closed.

Before the night was over I also invited three young men who had been staying there to join us. They all accepted! I figured it was only for a few weeks. Well, actually I didn't figure anything at all, at least until later. The thought of company, of such, in my mind, sophisticated and capable people sharing my home was exciting and comforting. I was struck by this unexpected opportunity biting at the heels of the previous day's plea to the universe. This could not be mere coincidence.

"Thank you," I whispered to whoever.

Phyllis Redman

Chapter 12

A Family

Leslie and her family took the room at the end of the chain of rooms that went from the kitchen into the living area, through an open space where I slept, to David and Robert's room at the rear. To the side of their room was one where Cindy had stayed, and now Leslie, Scott and Pahana. Anthony, Ed and Joe camped out in the living room. We were packed, but somehow it didn't feel crowded or uncomfortable. Each morning everyone cleared their space, while Leslie cooked a big pot of oatmeal and fruit. I was happy that she loved to cook. Not my forte, but I do like to clean up, so we were a good fit.

Anthony, Ed and Joe were quiet men who had been backpacking across the country and were charmed, as I, by Santa Fe, and decided to stay awhile. Anthony, who was from

Australia, was the most outgoing, entertaining us with colorful stories of his travels through the Outback, Europe and Africa. Ed and Joe were quiet, although Ed seemed more troubled than reticent. He reminded me of Mike, both in appearance and demeanor. The resemblance stirred my heart and I longed to comfort him in some way, but he didn't invite interaction, and spoke little about himself.

David and Robert were as happy as I to have this sudden family... and we felt like family from the first day. We flowed together easily, each of us doing whatever needed to be done without discussion. Dishes got washed, the bathroom cleaned, beds made, sleeping bags rolled up and stashed out of sight. I spent hours sitting cross-legged on the floor picking bits of dirt and pebbles from the white rug, listening to the conversation swirl around me, feeling safe and contented. I paid careful attention to these people whose lives were so different from mine, who seemed so vastly more capable than I of making their way in the world. I listened to their hopes and plans and observed their total absence of mind games or pretense.

I was especially interested in how Leslie and Scott parented Pahana, a cherub whose white-blond hair slid lazily around his wide, ruddy cheeks, whose smile constantly danced around his mouth as if laughter were the only natural state of being. They were so relaxed with him, addressing him with the same respect, the same tone they did everyone else. There was a sense of togetherness and cooperation I'd never experienced. They were all going in the same direction. Leslie had a sense of herself as a mother that reflected a confidence about what she was doing that I didn't have. I wanted to know how to believe in myself and my choices like that. I wanted to be able to give David and Robert a healthy self-esteem that would enable them to be as authentic and self-confident.

A week after this extended family filled my house, Leslie returned from town one afternoon waving a letter that had been sitting in her post office box for days. It was from her friend, Sus, who wrote to say that she and her family would be arriving in Santa Fe later that week. "Later that week" now meant any day. She and her partner were planning to set up a teepee a little south of the city, where they would stay for a time with her two young children.

"You'll love them, Phyllis," Leslie promised. "Sus was a Head Start teacher in Los Angeles and realized she'd rather be teaching her own kids than sending them to daycare for someone else to do it. So she quit her job, packed a few basics, and took off from the straight life. She and Larry have been traveling the southwest for months now, like us. We can all have Thanksgiving together. Gotta go tell Scott."

People living in a teepee, with children! I wondered if Sus questioned herself every inch of the way about what she was doing with her kids, as I did. Did she worry about them not attending school, getting sick, being different? Somehow I doubted it.

Phyllis Redman

Chapter 13

Giving Thanks

Thanksgiving morning I woke up in my tiny house crammed full of people, in the barrio of Santa Fe, New Mexico, excited and curious. A small astonishment shimmied across my consciousness at finding myself in this alien, magical place, thousands of feet above sea level, surrounded by Mexicans and Native Americans, piñon trees, turquoise skies and my happy, make-shift family. From wall-to-wall carpets and Danish modern teakwood to Thanksgiving in a teepee by a river. Was this really my life?

We all got up early, downed our oatmeal, and piled into either Scott's old station wagon or my little Honda Civic, and headed toward Cerrillos, an old ghost town nestled in the hills about fifty miles south of Santa Fe, where Larry and Sus had erected their teepee by the Cerrillos River. The sky, the soft grey of a dove's belly, hovered close to the mountaintops as we moved swiftly along the curving interstate, turning off after three quarters of an hour onto a narrow side road that twisted and dipped into a deserted town. It looked like a Hollywood set from an old western, complete with rolling tumbleweeds and the battered remains of old wood cabins with broken windows and crumbling front porches. The river lay minutes past town.

I'd seen Larry and Sus and the children a couple of times since they arrived. Sus was the quintessential California girl, blonde, tan and pretty without a stitch of makeup. Larry was equally the mountain man, full-bearded, handsome, with a handmade wool poncho thrown across his broad shoulders. They were a handsome couple. Sus' daughter Shasta, six, wore long skirts and had long, bouncing blonde ringlets, a little girl straight out of a Laura Ingalls Wilder story. Zev, four, was also blond and rosy-cheeked like Pahana. Robert's dark blond curls fit right in, but David, with his thick dark hair and eyes looked like he belonged with Scott, who was Mexican.

My heart was just plain happy at the sight of this small gaggle of children running along the edge of the river in the clean, crisp autumn air.

A big fire, shooting festive orange sparks toward the clouds, sat fifty or so yards from the two teepees. In it were dozens of big rocks heating to cook the turkey, which was stuffed into a huge pretzel tin and buried with some of the steaming rocks beneath and more piled on top. Larry periodically pulled them out as they cooled and replaced them with hot ones. The rest of the meal was cooking either over the outside fire or on the wood-burning stove in the center of the main teepee. I watched in amazement and contributed what I could, stirring the mashed potatoes and snapping the ends off the fresh green beans, imagining a life where every meal was prepared like this.

The turkey, which had been cooking since early morning, was ready late in the afternoon. After such a huge effort, we were all truly grateful for the fruits of so much labor. It was a real giving of thanks. I'd never understood gratitude the way I did at that moment. The peace I felt seeped into every nook and cranny of my being.

David, Robert and I slept with the other members of our household in the second, smaller teepee, although neither was actually small. A wood burner in the middle of the tent kept us warm through the night, but by morning it had gone cold. The teepee, when I awoke just after dawn, was freezing. My boys were snuggled together in their sleeping bags, cheeks rosy, hair tossed, angelic as only sleeping children can be.

Outside, the sky was lightening as I peed in the slight dusting of snow that had covered the dry riverbanks during the night. I was so moved by the beauty around me and the people who had welcomed us so generously into their world. I was alive and breathing in the world just as it was created! I looked at the ground below my feet, the sky over my head, the trees a short distance from the water's edge. No traffic, no sound at all other than the cawing of hawks as they swooped across the morning sky. No radio or television or machinery humming in the distance. Just my heart thumping peacefully in my chest.

Phyllis Redman

Chapter 14

Christmas Surprises

I knew it would be a Christmas like no other. Sus and Leslie suggested we make all our gifts. None of us had much money, and besides, they said, "Think how much fun it would be, how creative." Hmmm...

So the hunt for materials and ideas began. I designed and made blanket ponchos for the boys, and small pouches painstakingly beaded late at night after they were asleep. I was surprised by my own creativity, especially the pouches. That was something I'd never done before, and it wasn't easy. I also finished the sweaters I'd been knitting for them, a holiday tradition for years. Knitting was probably the only thing my mother taught me, and I'd been doing it a long time. All the children got pens, colored pencils, drawing tablets and some healthy treats. It really was fun and immensely satisfying.

Right before the holidays I got a note from the principal at David's school. "Mrs. L.," he wrote, "Your ex-husband called here and wants to talk to David. I need your permission."

This I hadn't foreseen. As much as I would have liked to sever all ties with Paul completely, I couldn't bring myself to cut my children off from their father. I'd let him know where we were as soon as we'd settled, and David had written to him several times. We didn't have a phone, or I would have let them call him. The distance provided a sense of security that vanished with this news. Even a phone call brought the fear right back, not just of Paul, but of myself and what I was doing. But how could I refuse? I knew the children missed him.

"There's something else," the principal continued, "that I think you should know. David is being bullied and generally having a hard time."

He described to me the general antipathy the other kids felt toward my son, just because he was white. Different. Shock shot through me like ice water swallowed too fast, leaving a painful lump in my throat. David had said nothing about this. When I hung up, I scribbled my permission for him to speak to his father and went into the bedroom where the children were playing. "Dave, can I talk to you for a minute?"

"Sure, mom." He eyed me curiously.

"What's going on at school? Are you having a problem with the other kids?" I asked him quietly.

He looked down and nodded.

"Why haven't you said anything?"

"I didn't want you to worry. I'm okay. I can handle it," he answered.

"What's going on? Have they hurt you?"

"Nah. Sometimes they push me a little, that's all."

I could see he wasn't going to say more, although I sensed he wasn't telling me the whole story. No, no way. This was not something I wanted my son to have to "handle." "There are only a few days until the holiday break. You can return to get your things and talk to your father and then you're never going back there."

His whole body relaxed.

"You should have told me, David. It's my job to worry. Don't you know I'd never want you to have to deal with something like that? Or see you hurt?"

I held him fiercely, until he wriggled away and happily bounced back into his room. How naive I was! How childishly idealistic! Not exactly the life-enhancing experience I'd hoped for.

No more school. Now what?

I had heard, in some of the discussions at *La Hermandad*, of a commune in Tennessee called The Farm. Occasionally someone passing through Santa Fe had been there or was planning a visit. I was intrigued by what I heard... a large hippie community in the middle of the state with a huge farming operation, a birthing center, and their own schools. David would be safe there, in the embrace of a gentle, peace-loving society. I thought about it a lot and eventually asked Leslie and Sus what they knew about it.

Sus said she knew a couple of folks who'd been there and thought it was a great place, modeled after the Israeli kibbutz, very family oriented. "Why? Are you thinking of going there?" she asked.

"Well, it's on my mind." I loved Santa Fe, the people who'd become family, the light, the surrounding mountains, the Plaza. The freedom! But Larry and Sus were planning to move on to a warmer place soon. (Winter was too hard in a teepee it seemed.) Leslie had mentioned visiting Scott's parents in Mexico. Anthony, Ed and Joe were definitely leaving after New Year's, headed for California. I'd been trying not to think about losing this family that I loved. I remembered how lonely I'd been. And now I needed to figure out what to do about school.

The world was tilting under my feet, threatening to dump me once more into an abyss of fear and loneliness. The closer we got to Christmas, the surer I was that I had to move on too. Leslie suggested that I take a day away to clear my head. "I'll look out for the boys, Phyl. Why don't you get in the car and head up to Taos for the day or something?"

I wanted to see Taos, home of Ram Das's Lama Foundation and *Be Here Now*. David and Robert were perfectly comfortable with Leslie and would be fine for the day. I got directions, hugged the kids, fueled up and hit the interstate again, this time headed north.

For a long time I drove through wide open plains, the Sangre de Cristo mountains lining the horizon to the west. Unlike the flat expanse of the Texas Panhandle, this space held me in a warm embrace, loosening the knots of anxiety that had been aching in my shoulders for the past few days. My breathing slowed and deepened. I hadn't been alone for four months. The quiet filled me, washing comfortably over my psyche. I yielded to the mesmerizing rhythm of my heartbeat, the gentle whirr of tires on blacktop, the commanding caw of soaring hawks in their graceful sweep across the sky.

Taos was exquisite, a tiny adobe town resting quietly in a small pocket surrounded by mountains. The light there, even more golden than in Santa Fe, reflected off the land like it was washed in Coppertone. The health food store, always the best source of information about local sites and happenings, was tucked into a slot along a small plaza. I got a chicken sandwich and some juice and stopped to chat with the clerk.

"So what's of interest around Taos? I'm just here for the day," I asked her.

Behind me, a young man with long, dark blond curls, jeans and a heavy poncho across his back, leaned over my shoulder. "There's a hot springs up in those hills there," he said, pointing to the south. "Gorgeous view, quiet. I'm headed there now. Want to tag along?"

"Sure. Is it far? I have to be back on the road around five."

It was forty-five degrees out. I'd just agreed to get in a stranger's truck to go soak in a steaming pool of water on the side of an orange mountain.

"Plenty of time. We can go in my truck. I'm Jack."

"Phyllis," I nodded, wondering for the umpteenth time if this were really my life and if I were completely insane to get into an old pickup truck with a total stranger and drive miles from another human being, into a strange world of treeless mountains and hot bubbling pools. The truth was, I wanted so much to find this world trustworthy and, so far, I hadn't been disappointed. I felt safer here than I'd ever felt on the tree-lined streets where I grew up. And so much less alone. The kindness and decency I'd encountered every inch of this journey were what I'd always been looking for.

Twenty minutes later, Jack parked his truck in a small clearing. We were high up the mountainside and had to climb down huge rocks the color of rust, holding on to their corners to keep from toppling over, until we reached a little pool tucked among them. Steam rose in waves above it. Jack began to peel off layers of clothing: the poncho, a heavy sweater, dark, long-sleeved tee shirt, undershirt, jeans, underpants. I hadn't thought about this part. Oh, hell, why not?

For two hours we soaked, up to our chins in eighty-five degree water, noses cold and sweat beading our foreheads. We talked about everything, our lives and loves, the war in Vietnam, music, God, our longing for a peaceful world. There was no sexual innuendo, no flirting and I was keenly aware of their absence. Who would have thought I could bathe naked with any man and not be hit on? Just as with the three men sharing my home, none of whom I'd slept with, I was learning the pleasure of male friendship and I liked it.

When the sun began to slide toward the horizon, we rose from the water, shivering and steamy as the cold air hit our hot bodies. I felt thoroughly cleansed and rejuvenated. The drive back to the plaza was silent and easy. When we got there, Jack helped me down from the high cab, embraced me gently, climbed back into the truck and disappeared before I shifted into drive.

Heading south, the mountains shadowing toward me as the sun continued its way toward the other side of the world, a deep peace surrounded me. Rested and renewed, my sense of purpose and energy restored, I was ready to deal with whatever was next. And I knew what that was.

I always loved Christmas despite my upbringing, and this one was the kind of celebration I'd always dreamed of: a house full of happy, excited children, a family gathered together. The gifts were surprisingly beautiful and useful, the collective creativity, awesome. Wrapping paper was everywhere, children were laughing and happy with their simple gifts, and Leslie made delicious egg and bacon burritos whose aroma filled the house and steamed the windows. David had spoken to Paul without dire consequence and had seen the last of his tormenters. Only the prospect of all this ending, which was imminent, shadowed the happiest Christmas morning I'd ever known.

Phyllis Redman

Chapter 15

The Hitchhiker

Two weeks after New Year's we left Santa Fe, with our hearts aching. I loved that place, where I found family, adventure, growth and courage. Anthony, Ed and Joe were gone, as were Sus and family. Scott and Leslie were leaving the next day. Cindy would no longer be nearby, and although I hadn't seen her much recently, she was my only link to home and was close and I knew it. I knew if I ever needed her, she'd be there. But that wasn't enough to stay when the rest of my "family" was moving on. As much as I wanted to stay, I also did not want to feel as alone as I had before.

Again the mystery of the unknown loomed ahead, exciting and scary. Cisco, the orange kitten who'd joined our family, mewed softly from David's lap. Once again Tucumcari's silent, barren presence surrounded us. This time, however, we stopped for lunch at the oddly-placed Chinese restaurant.

After we ate I handed David the keys and sent him and his brother out to the car while I paid the bill. As I pushed through the front door, it felt as if an invisible hand virtually shoved me to the side of the road, where a young man, puffed up like a balloon in a royal blue parka, stood with his thumb out. A huge backpack sat high on his shoulders, and wisps of red hair flew from beneath a knit cap.

"You want a ride?" I asked, before I had any idea I was going to speak.

"Sure. Thanks," he answered.

His name was Eric. The accent I discerned was from Brussels. He was one of five children, the only boy, his father was a milquetoast, and he was here to cut mama's apron strings. He was talkative, funny and passionate and I liked him immediately.

Hours later, as the sky darkened and a million stars appeared, we exited the interstate where a green sign said "lodging" and found a motel. We got one room with two king-size beds, one of which Eric and I shared. In the middle of the night, David and Robert sound asleep, Eric reached for me. We made a giggly, quiet sort of love after which I slept in his arms until morning.

Eric had no itinerary, just a vague idea of going east. I invited him to travel with us to The Farm, and he accepted. I had no idea how grateful I'd be for his presence when, hours later on the outskirts of Memphis, the Honda suddenly rattled a little, rolled a few yards in the dusky twilight, and, with a small cough followed by an ominous silence, simply stopped. I steered onto the shoulder, more than a little freaked out.

"I know some about cars," Eric said, "but I can't do nothing till morning. Can't see enough."

We settled back, the kids and I nervous, Eric calm as a pond on a windless night. Over-the-road semis, I discovered, traveled en masse at night, and every few minutes the little car was rocked by one whooshing by. My sense of safety suddenly vanished, replaced by a bizarre and illogical assortment of dark suspicions and anxieties. What if Eric was a serial killer? What if one of those huge trucks didn't see us and skidded into the car in the darkness? A UFO could touch down in the field beside us and spirit us away! Those thoughts actually ran through my mind, a complete 180 from the comfortable trust I'd been feeling just hours before, as I slipped into an uneasy sleep. Apparently I hadn't mastered the fearlessness of the people I'd been around at all.

When I awoke in the morning, Eric was already bent under the hood, pulling and pushing and rattling around. My fears evaporated with the darkness. After a half hour or so he poked his head around the hood toward the passenger seat.

"Spark plugs are dirty. Try the engine."

It sputtered a little and caught. My whole body relaxed. Where did that push toward Eric in Tucumcari come from anyway? What would I have done without him now, I wondered.

"That'll hold till we get to a shop," he said as he climbed back into the car. "Those plugs need to be changed. How long you been driving without a tune-up?"

Hell, it was a new car. Who'd thought about a tune-up? "Cross the country, a few months," I answered.

He snorted. "Women shouldn't have cars," he muttered.

In spite of myself, I just had to laugh.

The rest of the drive to The Farm was a blur of sunlight flashing through bare branches and bouncing off the newly-fallen, and rare, Tennessee snow. We were welcomed back east with a dazzling light show, not to be outdone by any Pink Floyd concert. Stephen's Farm, as it was known in hippie circles, sprawled over acres of lush southern farmland and forest. Founded several years before by Stephen and Ina May Gaskin, with a caravan of young people who were Stephen's students at San Francisco State College in Haight-Ashbury, it had grown from a dozen school buses full of hippies to over three hundred men, women and children who were in the process of creating a self-sustaining community based on Stephen's teachings. The intention was to be a peaceful, conscious and sustainable society.

The farming operation alone was a vast undertaking, the largest of a number of ambitious projects, including a shop to service cars and farm equipment, a general store, a school, a library and a birthing center. Ina May was a midwife who trained women from all over the country and ran a hospital where any woman could come to deliver her baby. She called her practice "spiritual midwifery," the title of the book she'd written.

Sus was accurate in her description of The Farm's social structure. Housing was by family unit, mostly in huge, old army tents where windows had been inserted and running water pumped in from wells. Unmarried men and women lived in tents also, dormitory style and separately. Bathing was in shower houses like the ones I remembered from overnight camp in the Poconos when I was a child. One outhouse served each dwelling, definitely not my favorite aspect of this lifestyle, although there was something to be said for shitting in the woods with birds chirping right over your shoulder and trees dancing above.

We were assigned housing with a young couple and told we could stay three days and then must either join the community or leave. I was certainly not going to make that kind of commitment after only three days. Joining entailed turning over all property, other than personal items, to The Farm. I knew right off I wasn't giving up my car. I now had to figure out plan B.

Although over three hundred people lived there, I rarely saw more than a handful at the same time, except on Sunday morning when dozens, including children, gathered in an open field for a spiritual service. We chanted the "Om," creating a palpable energy that felt like it could protect us from anything, like an energy firewall. Was this something that could save us if some idiot decided one day to push that nuclear button?

People were warm and friendly and looked me straight in the eye when we spoke. There was actually a Farm policy that strongly encouraged sustained eye contact, which could be warmly connective, but also quite disconcerting during a long conversation. Yet I'd be keenly aware of its absence in the outside world later. David and Robert were invited to attend Kid Herd, a daycare sort of activity, but open to children of any age. We spent a day at the school and spent hours around the wood-burning stove in the general store, an utterly quaint, small-townish place with rough wood floors and huge barrels full of pickles, potatoes and onions. In the cold weather, that was the social hub.

The three days passed quickly, barely long enough to formulate any kind of next step. At some point Eric asked me to marry him, a strictly business proposition he added. He needed to get a permanent green card because his visitor's visa was about to expire, and he wanted to stay here in the states. All I could think about was how hard it had been to get out of the last marriage, how much that piece of paper held me where I didn't want to be, all the legal bullshit to be free. Much as I liked him, trust was another thing entirely. I couldn't do it.

My thoughts turned to Barb, who was at Goddard College in Vermont. We'd sent reams of paper back and forth across the country since I left. Her descriptions of Montpelier and the little town of Plainfield, where Goddard is located, were charming. Maybe that was the place for us. I wrote Joan that we were coming back through Lansdale briefly and would love to see her and hang out for a few days. I wrote Barb that we were headed her way.

Eric accompanied us on the long drive back to Pennsylvania. Joan welcomed us with open arms and the boys were happy to be "home." But Heather and Josh had to go to school, and the days felt surreal, staying across from our old townhouse, yet no longer part of this life. David and Robert lazed around in front of the TV, eagerly awaiting Josh and Heather's return from school. Eric and I didn't do much more than the kids. My bones felt hollow and my nerve endings ached, yearning for a sense of belonging. The hours stretched out with nothing to do. After four days, we packed up yet again, consulted the road atlas that had guided us so far, and took another reluctant leave. I wanted to stay there, to come home, but I was driven to keep moving. How could I come back now? What was here for us? What had I accomplished? That would have felt like defeat.

"Will you reconsider, Mamatree? It's just for a year," Eric offered his proposal one more time, using the nickname he'd recently bestowed on me. "You branch out and mother everything in sight," he said the first time I heard it.

"I can't. I'm sorry," I replied, unable to overcome my fear of being trapped, of anyone having power over my life. As if I were doing such a great job of running it myself. Why did I want to do what I was doing alone? Writing these words now, I can only shake my head. What in the world was the matter with me? I liked him. What would it have been like if he hadn't been there when the car broke down? Was that a sign? Maybe not good reason to marry, but we weren't talking about romance, or even permanence. But how could I trust that? How could I trust anyone else when I didn't trust myself, at least when it came to making good choices? Such bravado! So foolhardy.

"So then goodbye. For now. Send your address to Joan when you have one in Vermont and I'll get it from her. We stay in touch. I go back to Iowa where I was, find a lady to sign the papers." He smiled wryly.

I wished him luck, my feelings tumbling around like clothes in a hot dryer. I didn't want him to go. I liked him. I didn't really want to do this alone, but I was too stubborn and pig-headed to give in. I concentrated on packing the car, aware of Joan's worried eyes following me about.

Chapter 16

Keeping on

Once more stuffed inside the little Honda, we rolled across the grey mid-winter afternoon, through Pennsylvania, New Jersey and into New York, headed to New England and the next stop of our odyssey. Cisco mewed angrily for a long time, not happy to be in the car again, turning himself around and around in the tiny space between the boys.

Snow started to fall sometime after three, progressing rapidly into a full-scale blizzard. The windshield wipers swatted ineffectually, with their rhythmic whap-whap, at the fat white blobs skittering across the glass. By dinner time I was afraid to keep going and found a motel right off the interstate. After a hot meal, we settled in for the night, feeling cozy and safe with the familiarity of television chatter humming as the children got ready for bed. Cisco prowled around, mewing forlornly.

"Mom," David asked suddenly, "where are we going now?"

"I told you, Vermont. Where Barb is," I replied

"Am I going to school there?"

"Of course. Do you want to go to school?"

He thought a moment, remembering Santa Fe no doubt. "Yeah, I guess. It would feel normal."

"Will I go to school too?" Rob piped up

"Um, don't think so, Robble-bobble. Next year you'll be old enough."

My son wanted to feel normal. I wasn't sure what that meant anymore, but I understood what he wanted, and his longing stung my heart. I was one of those snowflakes swirling in the wind, except I created that wind myself. I fell into a weary sleep, wishing Eric were there beside me.

I awakened to brilliant sunlight flashing through the blinds and bouncing onto the bed, like a pup eager for his morning walk. David and Robert tumbled out of sleep at the same time and rushed to the window.

"Mom," David said, "Where's the car?"

I rolled up the blinds and looked out. There were huge white mounds everywhere, across a world that was dazzling in the hard, yellow sun. The car was hidden within one of them.

We dressed and headed for the little motel restaurant for some hot oatmeal and toast, then went outside to wait for the plows that would allow us to be on our way. The kids were bundled stiffly into their heavy parkas, thick red mittens already coated with white. They immediately started building their first snowman of the season. David showed Robert how to pack the snow and roll it into a ball, in his best big-brother mode. Being cooped up in the backseat for hours had taken its toll on David's good nature, although he was usually a caring and attentive sibling. I watched them playing happily in the clean, cold sunshine, and I could only hope I was doing the right thing for them.

The snowman was only half done when the car was dug out and our overnight gear repacked. "Sorry guys, it's time to go. There'll be plenty more of this, believe me," I promised.

We arrived in Plainfield, a quaint little New England town, late in the afternoon. We'd landed in the middle of a Christmas card, silvery glitter and all. I'd never seen such a wintry extravaganza... Mother Nature in thick ermine wraps and twinkling diamond accessories, dazzling in the sun. For a moment we were silent, simply caught by her beauty.

Then we quickly found Barb, who'd been expecting us since the day before. It was so good to see her! Tomorrow she would help us find a place to stay, but for tonight we just pulled out our sleeping bags and camped in her small living room, catching up.

The next day we found an apartment halfway between Plainfield and Marshfield, another picturesque village a few miles to the north. The apartment was part of a motel that sat on a hill, looking like a weathered cherry overlooking miles of marshmallow topping. Over the motel's huge garage was a big, one room apartment that had two full-sized beds, a tiny kitchenette, a breakfast bar, two stuffed armchairs and a sunny bathroom.

"Layer up," Roger, the motel proprietor, told us. "Only way to stay warm in these parts."

I didn't take off my long johns, except to bathe, for the next three months.

Chapter 17

A World Of White

Winter in Vermont was relentlessly white. Houses had white siding, snow lay below, thick, pale clouds above. I felt stuffed inside a cotton ball. At first it was beautiful, then all too soon, muddy, grey and tiresome. All I wanted to do was stay in, especially when the sun was hidden behind those pale clouds, which it usually was. The days were slow and easy, and I didn't have much inclination to do anything. I was tired.

Occasionally we went into Montpelier to shop, and of course we were regulars at the health food store. People tended to be reserved in this quiet place, not unfriendly, but not particularly friendly either. New England hippies were different, reticent in a minding-my-own-business way. Eventually we did meet a few people and learn there were several small groups living communally nearby. Once in a while we were invited to stop by, which we did, but mostly I was content to hibernate. I was the she-bear, down for the winter with her cubs. Feeling safe and peaceful, I watched David trudge through the slush to the bottom of the long driveway, where a little yellow school bus picked him up each morning. He looked small and brave, which he was.

Through the big windows across the front of the apartment the pale sun washed over me, reading to Robert or watching him zoom his ever-present matchbox cars around the room. He was such an easy child, sweet and undemanding. My world was small and quiet and manageable. I gave myself a little time off from trying to figure anything out.

The boys were happy there. Although David didn't say much, he wasn't reluctant to go to school, and when asked, he promised it was really okay. The kids were nice, he liked the teacher and did his homework willingly. Rob eagerly awaited his brother's return in the afternoon, when they immediately rushed outside to enjoy the snow or ride on Roger's snowmobile. Roger and his wife, Nancy, had quickly become surrogate grandparents. The boys returned only when the afternoon shadows began to melt into dusk, their cheeks pink and eyes aglow.

By mid-February I began feeling queasy in the mornings. It took a few weeks for it to register. No, it couldn't be! Please, I thought, tell me I'm not pregnant! But the nausea didn't go away and of course I could be. Did I think of this possibility when Eric and I were together? Why didn't I use birth control? For goodness sake, I was a grown woman, not some hormone-addled teenager who didn't know any better.

Lost in the easy freedom of the moment, of the times, the possibility of getting pregnant may have flitted through my mind briefly but disappeared quickly. I wanted more children. I loved being a mom. But then? Could there have been a more inappropriate, more terrifying time for me to be pregnant? I was completely unsettled. I put off going to the Planned Parenthood in Montpelier. I didn't want confirmation, but I knew.

Not for a moment did I consider not having that baby, but I had no idea how I was going to manage. I was more alone than I'd ever been. I wrote to Eric, who'd sent his address to Joan to be forwarded to Vermont about a month before. He was back in Iowa, with a woman he "got to sign the papers." He responded to the news by telling me he had to stay where he was for a year to get his permanent visa. He'd stay in touch; he wrote that he had great faith in me. I guess I put on a good show.

One day a letter came from Paul. He knew where we were, as always, and the boys called him every now and then from Roger's phone. He was coming to see them the following week. Not a request; an announcement.

It was strange, a week later, to see him standing on the landing outside our door. He came in briefly, glanced around with obvious disapproval, and left with the boys. They were going to lunch and back to his motel in Montpelier. They'd be back at bedtime, he said, and I hoped that would be the case. I was pretty much a wreck until they returned, but return they did and, needless to say, I was relieved. They were sorry to see him go and it took some effort to comfort them and ease their homesickness. Although a few days later we were back to our easy rhythms, I wondered again what the hell I was doing. Was this fair to my children?

On into March I lazed through the days, shelving decision-making, ignoring the growing issue. I was so tired. Mornings were spent staving off the nausea, yoga breathing as I straightened up and tended to Robert. In the afternoons we went into town or took a walk, if it was sunny, or played games and read if not. When David got home, off they'd go until dusk, which was coming later every day. I'd glance out to check on them every so often; I could see a great distance across the road to the acres of largely untouched snow, laying like fresh sheets thrown across a lumpy mattress. The rule was they were to stay where I could see them. The only times they weren't visible were when they were off with Roger zooming around on the snowmobile. At least that had been the case, until one day in late March when they didn't appear when the sun began to slide toward the horizon.

Nancy answered when I knocked on the door. "Hey, Nance, is Roger out with the kids on the snowmobile?" They usually told me if they were going with him.

"No, he's in here. Didn't take it out today."

"Have you seen them? They're usually home by now and I can't see them." Now I was worried.

"Roger, have you seen David and Robert?" Nancy called into the house.

Roger appeared quickly, frowning. "No, not since yesterday."

Now we were all anxious. Roger got his coat, told me to stay at the apartment in case they came back, and headed out to the garage. Moments later we saw the snowmobile slicing down the hill, following the little boot tracks in the snow.

I climbed the stairs to our apartment and stood on the tiny platform outside the door. I could see for miles it seemed, and there was no sign of two little boys in bright blue jackets. The knot in my stomach was nothing like the upset I had each morning. This was an encompassing cramp tightening like a vise throughout my entire body, a huge fear that left no room for breath. There could be ponds under all that snow, possibly thin ice that wouldn't be visible until too late. Where could they be that I couldn't see them?

What seemed like a long time passed. I could see Nancy peer out the window every few minutes, her face worried and pale. I was frozen with fear, praying to see them on their way back safely. When at last I saw the snowmobile coming over a small hill, it was too far away to see if Roger was still alone. I saw two small blue dots beside him only when he was nearly to the road. I almost collapsed with relief. Nancy opened her door and waited just inside the kitchen, smiling.

I came down the stairs and grabbed them both, thanking Roger with a great deal of passion. He just smiled and nodded, then took the snowmobile into the garage. David and Robert had no idea why I was holding on to them like a drowning person, why there were tears on my cheeks.

"Don't you ever, ever, ever do that again," I exploded, when the fear subsided enough to speak coherently. "Don't you ever go so far from the road or behind hills where I can't see you. You know better. You don't know what's out there, under the snow. You promise me right now."

"Gee mom, we're okay. We were right on the other side of that hill there," David said, pointing to a large rise a good distance away.

"Not where I can't see you. You got that? Both of you. Robert?"

They nodded, David just a little annoyed I could tell. Well, too bad.

The second week in April brought us into what Vermonters call "mud season." The world turned from white to brown, which was a welcome change. There was no doubt by then that I was pregnant, confirmed weeks before by the doctors at Planned Parenthood. I had to make some decisions. We couldn't stay indefinitely in a one-room apartment. I had little income, just the small amount Paul had, thankfully, continued to send, and what was left of the money my father left. I had virtually no support system here, other than Barb, who was busy with her studies and college life. What were my options? I could return to the Farm, where pregnant women could stay until their babies were born or go back to Lansdale. Back to my mother, with whom I'd exchanged only a few letters, and Paul, an option that didn't appeal to me at all. Or we could get an apartment here.

A week after mud season began there was an immense storm, blanketing the world once more in white. That made up my mind in a snap. Enough. We packed the car, said another reluctant goodbye to Roger and Nancy, and headed into Plainfield for one last breakfast with Barb. We were going back to Tennessee, to the spiritual midwives at The Farm, and a whole new birthing experience.

Chapter 18

Don't Fence Me In

We left winter behind quickly, progressing from white to brown to green as the miles rolled away. The open windows brought in cool spring air to revive us. What a relief! After an overnight stop at Joan's once again, we reached Tennessee two days later. This time the vista was a riot of pink and white and a hundred shades of green. Yellow dandelions and buttercups dotted the ground, and the air carried the sweet scent of honeysuckle.

Just at the entrance to The Farm, a small cabin displayed a welcome sign that requested all visitors stop and sign in. I told them I was pregnant and wanted to deliver my baby under Ina May's care. We were assigned housing with a different young couple and their two-year-old daughter, Guinevere. There was a double bed for the boys and a narrow daybed for me. A small space, set off by a wide countertop, had a sink with running water that was pumped in from a well outside. A wood-burning stove, between the kitchen area and the living quarters, served for heating and cooking. In the far corner beside a double bed for her parents was Guinevere's crib. The large tent had curtains on the built-in windows and was homey and comfortable.

After unpacking the personal items we'd need daily, the boys and I went for a walk, carefully marking signposts and "street" signs along the way so we could find our way back. There were dozens of trails angling off the main thoroughfare, leading to other tents, a few newly built or under construction wood houses, the general store, the school, the library and the stream. Most of these places were marked by small, rough wood signs.

Along the way we were greeted by several people passing by on the road or working outside their homes. One woman was hanging laundry out to dry, her children's small shirts flapping in the breeze. Everyone was friendly and made unblinking eye contact. "Was I new to The Farm?" they asked, nodding when I said I was there to deliver my third child. They were warm and welcoming to David and Robert, sometimes inviting them to come play with their own children.

We slipped easily into life there. David went to the little school until it closed in late May so that the older children could help with planting season. Robert went to Kid Herd, which he loved, so happy that he could go to "school" too. Sometimes I stopped by to watch the young teachers, in their long calico skirts, leading the littles in a song or supervising some playground activity.

One day someone asked if I'd like to set up a library. There were boxes and boxes of donated books sitting in a shed near the school. I spent an hour or two a day going through them, sorting by genre. I was always happy around books.

Occasionally a bunch of us piled into an old school bus and rode a short distance down the road to pick wild strawberries, tiny and dark red to their centers, nothing like the big, tasteless berries at the supermarket. They tasted like swallowing the sun. I learned to make tortillas from scratch, mixing corn meal and water into a gritty dough, which got rolled out and baked on an old cookie sheet in the wood-burner. I even chopped wood and got the burner started, gathering kindling from the abundance in the surrounding forest. The physical activity brought my body to life after the sedentary winter. Other than when it rained, we were rarely indoors, probably walking several miles a day. The Honda, parked in a clump of bushes near our tent, was practically growing roots. The love of nature born in those woods has never left me.

Once a week the clinic was open, offering regular check-ups for the many pregnant women. A doctor came from nearby Summertown once a month. That's where I met Mimi, another young mother with a five-year-old son and a baby due in September, a month before I was due. Mimi was a quiet farm girl from Iowa, with thick, dark hair that fell like a velvet curtain to her waist. She drove a flaming red pickup truck, which, she said, she'd never give up. I could relate. We bonded instantly.

Food was problematic. We arrived in the early spring, when provisions from the previous year's harvest were worn thin and the spring crops hadn't yet come in. We ate a lot of potatoes, cabbage and onions, soy burgers, corn meal mush in the morning, and tortillas and peanut butter, a luxury reserved for pregnant women and children, for lunch. The Farm was strictly vegan, so the only milk was soy. In fact, butter, milk, burgers and ice cream were all made from the hard to digest beans. They said that if you slaughtered six cows, they would provide food for sixty people, but the soy beans that fed those cows could feed a village. In fact, The Farm had received a couple of international awards for their work with soy products.

When my sons complained, about six weeks into our stay, that they were hungry, and asked if we could go into town for some burgers, it sliced my heart open like a ripe melon. It wasn't that they weren't getting enough to eat, they were just tired of potatoes and peanut butter and cornmeal mush. But hearing my kids even say those words was painful. How does the mother of a truly starving child bear it?

Mimi said her son had the same complaint, so we decided it was time for a trip into town to the local diner. However, when I mentioned it to our hosts, they reminded me that we had to sign out. Only a limited number of people per day could leave The Farm and go into town. That had been explained when we first arrived, but I'd forgotten. Although there was a good reason, that didn't sit well with me or Mimi. We had to wait a week before there was a day open for us.

From what I heard, it took years for the local townies to accept the wildly dressed, long-haired people into their midst. In time the locals were won over by the solid work ethic and gentle ways of the hippies, but no one at The Farm wanted to risk overwhelming the people of Summertown with hordes of them descending at the same time on the small town. Hence the limit. Never one to take kindly to restrictions of any kind, that was the beginning of my disenchantment.

The Farm should have been my ideal place. There was the kindness, integrity and respect I longed for and a society where everyone shared the same beliefs. They lived close to and in tune with nature. There was shelter from the mean and greedy outside world that I was fleeing. It was a world I should have felt at home in, but for some reason didn't. I liked my creature comforts. And familiarity. I was not willing to relinquish my car or my attachments. Was it worth the price? I think it was... but I wasn't ready to pay it. I was too rooted in habit, too attached to a lot of things. Too unwilling to compromise. I admired those people, honored them, wanted to be like them, but I wasn't. I felt restless, hemmed in, uncertain. I didn't trust myself or my ability to make good choices and therefore I didn't believe completely in what I was doing. There'd been so many voices for so long telling me I was wrong. They chattered in my mind and burrowed into my soul, louder and more powerful than either my longing or my rebelliousness.

By late May, Mimi and I were both feeling caged in. Too many rules and too much restriction. I never considered The Farm anything but a wonderful place. Just not my wonderful place. I wanted to pee in a real toilet, eat a ham sandwich, take a ride to the corner drugstore when I felt like it. I was uncomfortable denying my kids those things.

I longed for a conversation that didn't always require unrelenting eye contact, which seemed as contrived and distancing as refusing to look at someone directly. After many long hours discussing the pros and cons of living there, Mimi and I both decided to leave. It scared me silly to think of returning to Philadelphia. I would have to go, at first, to my mother's. Me and my two long-haired kids and my swelling belly. This was not going to be pretty.

Chapter 19

Now We Are Four

My mother was not happy to see me, the daughter who did nothing right. What would the neighbors think when they saw this strangely dressed child of hers, with her two long-haired sons and big belly? How could I do this to her? She shrank me like a wool sweater mistakenly thrown into the dryer.

Exhausted, confused and scared, I did all I could to show a happy, confident face to David and Robert until Paul took them for their week at the shore. I'd forgotten what it felt like to have time alone and pretty much collapsed for a few days, hiding in my mother's second bedroom or walking the tree-lined streets around her apartment house, defeated and disoriented. I'd become used to smiling faces and all that eye contact. Now, other than curious or openly denigrating glances, no one looked at me. Although the nearby homes were green and beautifully landscaped, I could almost feel the earth smothering under all that concrete. Car exhaust stung my nostrils.

By the beginning of July, looking to resettle back near Lansdale, I started making phone calls. Few of my old friends were still there, most having gone out west and, wisely, stayed there. Joan, I quickly found out, was leaving for Minnesota shortly, where her fiancé had been transferred. It dawned on me slowly that I wasn't returning to anything. This was a whole new ballgame, a world that felt almost as foreign to me as Santa Fe once had.

By August we'd settled into a two-bedroom apartment in a small garden complex on the edge of Lansdale. We were in a corner unit on the ground floor, with a small patch of trees right outside through which David and Robert, who would begin half-day kindergarten that September, could walk to the school just on the other side. I loved those trees.

I had to ask Paul to co-sign the lease, which he did reluctantly. I felt trapped between two worlds, refusing to get a telephone or a TV, holding on tightly to pieces of the life I'd been living for the past year. Crazy and impossible to live in both realities at once, I nonetheless gave it my best shot. Like the monkey who can't get the rice out of the jar because his closed hand is too big to get through the opening, I kept my fist clenched tightly, unable to commit myself in any one direction.

The baby was due early October. School began and the days settled into an easy rhythm. I picked Rob up at noon and we spent the afternoons taking walks into town or at the playground in the center of the complex. He loved the big sliding board, pure joy on his face as he swooshed downward, his hair flying out behind his little freckled face, eyes aglow. "Look, mommy, look," he'd call to me, and beneath my hand

114

the new baby would roll over as if joining in on his big brother's fun. Whatever may have been out of sync in my life, there was nothing that marred those happy moments.

I began weekly visits to a birthing center staffed by midwives, the only one of its kind in the Philadelphia area. An old friend of Barb's, whom I'd met several times, took me under her wing and volunteered to be my coach during delivery. Charlotte, who was more than ten years older than I, lived minutes away on an old farm where she boarded horses to make enough money to keep her land. She was a sculptress and lived in a small studio/apartment on her property, while she rented out the big, white colonial just yards away. I loved to visit, helping occasionally to feed the horses. David loved them too and sometimes got to ride one around the property, but Robert found their size intimidating, clinging to my hand and pressing his face against my leg.

My water broke one sunny afternoon as I sat on the front steps outside, watching Robert furiously pedal his Big Wheel up and down the driveway. I called to my neighbor, a friendly, middle-aged woman in the apartment above ours, who allowed me to use her phone when I needed to make a call. "Joyce, it's time," I yelled up to her window. "I think my water just broke. Can you call Charlotte for me?" She'd been expecting this and had Charlotte's number.

"Oh my," Joyce answered. "Right away." As soon as she called, she came out and sat beside me until Charlotte arrived, just minutes later. Charlotte quickly grabbed my packed overnight bag and Robert, and hustled us into her car, calm and efficient in contrast to my complete collapse of nerve. "I've changed my mind. I don't want to do this," I muttered all the way to the birthing center.

"A little late in the game, I think," Charlotte laughed.

Booth Maternity Center was a small stone building on the campus of Saint Joseph's University on the other side of the city. Surrounded by tall old trees, it was a serene place, somehow quiet and undisturbed by the traffic whizzing by on City Line Avenue. Charlotte pulled up to the large glass front door and ran in to get someone. A young woman came out with a wheelchair, helped me out of the car and pushed me inside while Charlotte parked the car. By the time she and Robert came in, a few moments later, I was ready to go upstairs. Robert, looking pensive, stayed close to Charlotte as we took the elevator to my room.

"Hey, Robble-bobble, you're going to have a little brother or sister very soon," I said, smiling at him and opening my arms. He came into them hesitantly. "It's okay, sweetie, I'll be home in a couple of days. Your dad's going to pick you up soon and then you're gonna get David. You'll stay with daddy till I get home," I explained. He held onto me for a moment, then took Charlotte's extended hand, looking back for a moment before they walked out the door. I saw her put her arm around his shoulders and pull him close.

I winced as a contraction washed over me, and the midwife leaned over to rub my back. What a far cry from the sterile, glaringly-lit experience of my first two deliveries, surrounded as I was now by women, all of them bustling about like a room full of mothers preparing their children to go on stage for a school play. I distracted myself by observing the red and orange foliage in the window, lit up by the sun setting behind it, like a celebration of the event unfolding within.

The contractions were sporadic, appearing and disappearing much as my fears were. I wanted this baby, certainly, but how was I going to manage? I'd kept the worry away so far, but now it popped its distraught face up between contractions, when my body and mind were not absorbed with breathing, like someone on the other end of the seesaw I was bouncing on, with no control whatsoever.

As evening darkened the room, the midwife appeared and sat down on the bed beside me. "How're you doing, Phyllis?" she asked.

I glared at her. "Just swell."

"Yes, well, I'm going to give it till morning," she said. "This little being is in no rush to make an appearance, it seems. We don't want to risk infection, with your womb wide open like it is. If you haven't progressed significantly, we'll just give you a little jump start tomorrow. You're only three centimeters dilated at this point."

Fourteen hours later, after a dose of Pitocin, Jason was caught by the same young midwife, cleaned up and laid beside me. He looked exactly like a creased version of his father. We were left to bond, someone checking in every ten minutes or so. Charlotte sat beside me reading, when she wasn't bent over Jason's tiny head, with its sprinkling of reddish-blond hair, cooing softly to him. I was tired and happy as I held the warm weight of my third son against my chest. It had not even occurred to me to call Eric.

How had I forgotten how exhausting a new baby is? Although he was a calm, easy baby, there were still feedings every few hours, little sleep and two older children to care for.

Charlotte fixed meals for us and came by every day the first few weeks, but I dragged through the days, limp as a forgotten pansy. My mother visited a few times a week, always accompanied by a litany of criticism and reproach. Her scowling face was not comforting, but she did distract David and Robert for a little while so I could rest, and even she softened for a newborn. Jason's smile was sunshine warming us all on those chilly, autumn afternoons.

I was more than grateful when a letter arrived from Barb in mid-November saying that she would be coming back to Lansdale in December until the summer, doing an off-season semester toward her degree from Goddard. She planned to stay with us, if I wanted. Oh yes. Once more my needs had been met and I was grateful;. Once again, I was rescued.

Chapter 20

A Season of Calm

December eighteenth was Robert's birthday. Not only was I bone weary, but I also had some sort of bug that had me doubled over with stomach cramps. Refusing to let that interfere with the celebration I'd planned for him, I didn't cancel the dinner invitation to his father and new stepmother. It was for my son and I thought it would make him happy, so I put aside any fears that Paul was still someone who could hurt me, that it was better to keep him at a safe distance. He would not look with a kind eye at my sparse, hippie-style decor, at the bright red Indian bedcover thrown across the cot that served as a makeshift sofa, or the beaded curtain that hung between the front door and the living room.

That afternoon I bundled Robert and Jason into their winter gear and headed for the Acme across the street, bent at a right angle as I pushed the stroller, Rob's mittened hand tucked into mine against the handlebar. I prepared dinner the same way, sweat beading my forehead, stomach cramped like an angry fist. For someone with a Rhodes Scholar Letter of Commendation I was really idiotic sometimes. So determined to live by what I believed, to be generous because I valued generosity, I completely ignored life's warning signals, and just plain common sense, over and over again.

Dinner was strained, but Robert was happy to have us all together. I saw Paul looking around the room, eyes resting on some photographs on the wall that Barb took for a school project, when I was pregnant with Jason. Once again, heedless of the danger of Paul's narrow mindset, which was far closer to the norm than mine, I forgot that I was only partially clothed in some of them. I made a deliberate effort to teach my children that nudity was a natural, unremarkable state. I didn't want them to always associate nudity with sex no matter what the world told them.

A week later Barb arrived, bringing with her the aroma of fresh-baked whole wheat bread, which we ate in warm, thick slices covered with cream cheese and apple butter. Barb was very social, upbeat and fun-loving and the apartment was suddenly filled with company and conversation, like the days after my divorce. The kids got lots of attention and loved it. As did I.

We glided over the ice of winter quietly, the days filled with all the simple, ordinary activities of life with children: getting them off to school in the morning, cleaning, laundry, walking through the trees with Jason in his stroller to pick Robert up at noon, homework in the evenings, and the sweet bedtime rituals of snuggling and reading favorite stories, my most treasured moments of the day. Rob loved *Norman The Doorman*, about a mouse whose cozy little hole in the wall was the ultimate homey, filled with tiny, plumply stuffed armchairs, little lamps casting a golden glow and a roaring fireplace. David's special book was *The Diggingest Dog*, about a dog who wanted to learn to dig so he'd be like all the other dogs. Clear what was on their minds, I thought as they pressed close to me, Jason tucked between us, at the close of day. I still have those books.

For the moment I was content. Each day with Jason brought a new accomplishment... a first smile, discovering a foot, finding his thumb. He awakened in the morning and always turned his head toward the sound of the birds' singing, which earned him the nickname Jake Littlebird. I watched him and thought, this time I'll do it right. No hurtful divorce, no back and forth tug of war between parents. This child would know love and peace. No threat of loss hanging over my head. This time I would create a happy world for all my children. But the old yearning for a family, for a community, lay dormant, like a snake ready to strike, especially on holidays when I had no family for my children to celebrate with. I knew when Barb left the loneliness would return.

Eric kept in touch but showed no inclination to see his son or to send any money. Nor did I suggest he chip in. I rarely asked anyone for anything, at least not willingly, not because of any notion of self-reliance or goodness - this had been my decision after all - but because I felt no sense of connection to anyone. Which isn't to diminish all the help I received along the way from the caring and generous people I met. But I insisted on carrying all responsibility alone, no matter how exhausting or lonely, as I always had, perpetuating my loneliness without the slightest idea I was doing so.

But actually, I wasn't the only one responsible. A friend pointed that out to me many years later. Why was it that I, like so many others, held only the woman accountable for what two people had done? I've never heard anyone criticize an unwed father. In fact I never held anyone else accountable for anything. In my mind, only I was responsible for the unhappiness in my marriage. Clearly I'd bought into this belief, not only where Jason was concerned, but across the board.

Over the months I stayed in touch with Linda, from *La Hermandad*. In the early spring she wrote to say that she and Bob, with whom she had a two-year-old little boy, were in West Virginia and getting married in late June. She'd love it if we came, she wrote, and Barb was welcome too.

"Well, what do you think?" I asked Barb, who'd been hearing all along about the colorful cast of characters I'd met over the past year and a half.

"Love to. I don't have to be back in Vermont until August," she answered.

So began the final leg of my travel adventures. The end of one chapter, the start of a wretched and unexpected one. This past year would be the last happy one for a very long time.

Two weeks before we were to leave I traded my two-year-old Honda Civic for an old VW minibus that had a bed in the back, perfect for traveling with three young children. That was what I told myself, even while wondering about the wisdom of such an exchange. I loved the Honda, and it was practically brand new.

When school ended, we packed up the apartment, intending to find another when we returned. If we returned. There was that disruptive little demon again, whispering, "Keep looking."

Phyllis Redman

Chapter 21

Mountain Mama

John Denver aside, as far as I was concerned the country roads of West Virginia were far more hellish than heavenly. True, they were beautiful, edged by dense woods with little sign of human interference. However, they twisted and turned, rose and fell, like snakes climbing over one another, creating huge, dark hills with limited visibility. Judging by what we'd seen so far, I figured there wasn't six feet of straight, flat roadway in the entire state.

The night we drove across the state line, the sky was, at first, speckled generously with stars, clear and bright in the absence of any man-made light. The state highway curved and dipped and curved some more, our headlights the eyes of some slowly moving sci-fi creature cutting through the midnight forest. The boys slept on the bed that sat atop a large storage bin filled with our supplies for the summer. The emerald-green carpeted van, so perfectly hippie, made me feel for the moment that I was really a member of the counterculture I so admired.

I loved the van, at least until it stalled in the middle of the night, at precisely the same moment that thunder began to rumble across the heavens and lightning rip furiously through the darkness. The storm was brief and fierce. The sharp bolts slammed into the paved surface around us and cracked off the top branches of a huge tree not nearly far enough away. Barb and I were terrified. I was grateful I wasn't alone. The boys somehow, miraculously, remained asleep. Robert would have been petrified I knew. Eventually Barb and I dozed off too, slumped at odd angles across the bucket seats, at a dead stop in the middle of the road.

When we awakened, the sun filtered in lacy patterns through the masses of huge, old trees, and the sky was clear and blue. Warm air softly washed away the slight chill of the night, taking with it our fear. We surveyed our predicament and were happy to see that we were, fortunately, at the very top of a long hill curving downward into a beautiful valley. Not one other car had gone by since we stalled there. David and Barb, who was resourceful and deceptively strong for all her five feet, three inches, managed to push the van enough for me to pop the clutch and get the engine running. We didn't stop again until we reached Parkersburg, well past our destination, but the closest city where we could be pretty sure of finding someone to service a VW. We came to a small auto repair shop at the edge of town where a mechanic was just opening up, steaming coffee cup in hand.

"Yer starter's bad," he told us after what seemed like only a minute. "Yer lucky, I got one here that'll work. Run ya about a hunnerd twenty bucks."

Swell. "Okay," I sighed, "do it."

It took about an hour, just long enough to get some breakfast, and we were on our way again. Mid-afternoon we reached Bob and Linda's mailbox, propped at an angle by the highway, Queen Anne's lace winding around the post like a royal collar. A wide, muddy dirt path stretched behind it into the forest, where an oversized van was running shuttle from the paved road to the cabin. The driver waited for us to climb into the back, where several other wedding guests were already seated on low benches lining the inside walls of the vehicle. Our feet rested on the hot floor, a dozen flower children wilting in the early summer heat of the windowless van.

Because of the rain the night before, what passed for a road was a thick, muddy swamp that caught us in its sodden grip. The driver revved and revved, and we rocked and rocked, to no avail. My feet were on fire, right through my rubber flip-flops. David was pale and we were all drenched with sweat. Robert held tightly to my hand and Jason sucked frantically on his binky.

Eyes scrunched shut, I gathered all my concentration and pictured the tires disengaging from the muck. I did this for maybe three minutes and damned if we didn't suddenly pitch forward and get on our way. Did I have anything to do with that or was it just a fortunate serendipity? My sense of reality was slightly skewed by then, so I wasn't sure, but what a relief!

Linda greeted us with her wide, sweet smile, glowing in a long patchwork skirt and white peasant blouse, her sleek hair tied back with fresh daisies. Bob also wore a full, white peasant shirt, billowing loosely over his jeans. His full beard and thick, curly hair haloed his face against the sun. Dozens of people dotted the rolling green lawn... young men and women with scrubbed faces, barefoot children, even a handful of locals in starched white shirts and pale, flowered dresses, carefully tended roses in a garden of wildflowers.

Bob and Linda had written the ceremony themselves, after giving the whole idea of marriage a lot of thought. At one point after arriving in West Virginia, they'd almost split. "He wants to open the relationship, Phyl," Linda wrote, "to include another woman he's attracted to. I don't think I'm comfortable with this, but I have to think about it."

Was she kidding? Think about it? Seriously? Did that ever really work? But the whole community got involved in a surprisingly serious and honest dialogue that resulted in Linda deciding she was not open to it... and here they were. No anger. No recrimination. No resentment. Attraction happens, no matter how much you love someone. Sort of a collective, though not indifferent, shrug. This was the kind of world I wanted to live in. My idea of civilized.

The cabin was small, so Linda arranged for the five of us to stay with a young man named Nick who had a small farm about fifteen minutes away. We were there almost a month, visiting Linda frequently and getting to know the hippies who'd settled in the hollows. Many young people had worked in the cities to make enough money to buy land, which was relatively cheap here.

They were a colorful cast of characters, to say the least. Nick was surprisingly young, in his early thirties, to have retired on a hundred and fifty acres of rich West Virginia soil, where vast cornfields surrounded a beautiful old farmhouse. Trader Johnny, down the road, had boxes upon boxes of old buttons, arrowheads, polished stones and other artifacts that fascinated my kids. He and his wife, Lady Susan, had three young daughters and the five children played together for hours when we visited.

Susan made colorful patchwork skirts and calico blouses with ribbons sewn across the front and hanging down, Indian style. I bought a three-tiered skirt of calico patches, a long-sleeved, wine-red blouse, and, at a flea market nearby, a half dozen applewood buttons made by another local craftswoman. West Virginia is home to hundreds of men and women known nationally for their excellent craftsmanship, which we got to see at several local craft shows and flea markets. There were rocking chairs made from long twigs, soaked in water and then curved into half circles and curlicues, quilts in bright looped colors, all kinds of clothing, and farm implements that were worthy of pedestals in Americana museums. A knitter for years, my fingers itched for some richly hued yarns and a pair of needles in my hands. And there was food! Homemade pies and jams, cakes and sausages, corn relish and pickles, none of which tasted anything like their store-bought counterparts.

The end of July the boys and I moved to Bob and Linda's, while Barb stayed at the farm with Nick. Every afternoon we picked veggies from the garden for dinner and my love of working with the land resurfaced. Watching the small tomatoes emerge from their yellow bonnets, and the tiny, perfectly formed peppers sprouting from their white ones, satisfied my soul completely. Wherever I ended up the next summer, I wanted a garden.

David and Robert collected fresh eggs each morning from the hen house, which was their favorite place to play. They'd named every chicken, and one day, both holding one of my hands while I propped Jason on the other hip, they dragged me out to the front lawn and introduced me to every single one of those squawking birds! They spent hours chasing them around, inventing games I didn't understand. With electricity, and therefore no television, their imaginations were in high gear.

We bathed in a little pond a few hundred yards from the cabin, soaping up and rinsing off on its banks, then jumping into what felt like recently melted ice for a final rinse. In the sultry heat, the cold of the water was a surprise. What would it be like in winter, I wondered. Bathing outdoors and peeing in a teepee-covered outhouse atop a small hill, looking out over the richly green hollow, might be tolerable in summer, even charming, but not a particularly appealing prospect in the cold, no matter how breathtaking the view was.

My longing for the peace, the freedom, and the decency of those people was at war with my attachment to the creature comforts I was used to. I briefly considered renting a place nearby, not terribly far from the cabin, and even looked at a small house for rent that was situated along the paved highway nearby. But although it boasted indoor plumbing and electricity, not a given in these parts, there were no neighbors within sight. I was not brave enough, not ready to give up the sense of safety I felt from the proximity of other people, although I was well aware that this security could be an illusion in a world where next door neighbors went months without seeing each other, and sometimes didn't know each other's names.

There was a woman who lived down a dirt road, deep in the hollow, whose husband walked out on her and their two little boys. She had no car. Every single day someone went down that road and checked on her. This was a real community. At home, would anyone even walk across the street to check on me? I wouldn't count on it. I knew this. As a single mom with three children, I also knew that I didn't want to wake up one night, alone with a sick child, and the nearest person a mile or more away. Probably without a phone.

I was reaching for a world that would welcome me and my kids and offer us some sense of family... and there it was. I knew I would not be left alone on holidays. My children would be cared about. Could this only be found in these hollows, or the fields of Tennessee, or the counterculture of Santa Fe? At least for those of us with no family support? Why did I keep pushing myself toward a lifestyle that I was either not ready, or not the person for? I understood how Hamlet felt... to be there or not.

Loneliness was steering the ship, idealism its first mate. I could not make peace with who I was because I was not who I wanted to be.

My mind was made up when Robert came down with a mild case of dysentery from the well water at the cabin. Every few hours Linda and I rushed him to the outhouse, all day and through the night, Linda guiding us with a big flashlight, me carrying my little boy. I was totally freaked out, although Linda didn't find it alarming at all. "Lots of folks get this until their bodies adjust to the local bacteria," she soothed me. Maybe. But I couldn't do this.

"Ruin is the road to transformation."

-Elizabeth Gilbert, *Eat Pray Love*

Chapter 22

Shattered

I returned to Pennsylvania early on the morning Paul planned to leave for the shore on his summer vacation with the kids. The air was still cool, the sun slowly drying up the dew as I dropped them off at his door on the way to my mother's. He was furious that I was so last minute.

"Where should I bring them back to?" he asked tersely.

"I told you they'd be here on time. I'll be at my mother's until I find an apartment. Call me there when you get back," I answered just as coldly, knowing I was being just plain bitchy. It wasn't like me. He wasn't wrong to be annoyed. And he did co-sign our lease. But then he turned and crouched for the boys to jump into his arms, which they were too big to still be doing. They'd tried to tell him they didn't want to do that anymore, but he ignored them. "Be daddy's good boys," he crooned. And so they awkwardly complied, while I seethed with anger, watching him do to them what he'd always done to me... refuse to hear anything he didn't want to hear. Not care what I felt or what I wanted. I remembered why I was so different, so unpleasant with him. As usual I drove away feeling uneasy, a dark cloud planting itself above by head until they were safely back.

My mother was expecting me, just as unhappy to see me as she'd been the year before. "Well, what are you going to do now? You have to find a place to live. I can't help you, you know," she greeted me.

Well hello, and how are you too. "Yeah, I know, mom. Believe me, I don't expect it." Even as I said the words, I wondered how I would get a lease in my name unless Paul co-signed again. Would he? I hated being dependent on him and was well aware that my life was way out of control. What was I doing? I had no right to expect others to take on my responsibilities. I didn't want them to, but right then I didn't know what else to do other than what I was doing.

I rationalized that everything I'd done was justifiable. Why shouldn't a mother seek the best possible world for her children? Wasn't that what I'd been doing? Would anyone raise an eyebrow if I were a man whose job opportunities took him from place to place? The boys were fine. We'd had remarkable experiences and met wonderful people. And now I was tired of running, of seeking something I couldn't seem to stay with even when I found it. My kids were tired too. I kept coming back to where I started. Whether I didn't trust my judgment enough to commit to a totally different way, or I simply wasn't ready, didn't matter now. Maybe this was where I belonged. I didn't know. I didn't know much at that point, except that I was ready to stop.

It didn't take many phone calls to realize that without Paul's help it was unlikely I could rent a place. I had no number to call him, so I spent the days tending to Jason, walking, resting and stewing in my own overcooked juices, pulled apart like Texas barbecued pork.

The evening before David and Robert were due home, there was a knock on the door as Jason and I were about to settle in for bedtime stories. Two tall men in black leather jackets filled the doorway. I opened it hesitantly.

"Are you Phyllis Redman?" one of them boomed, much more loudly than could possibly have been necessary, his eyes focused somewhere over my right shoulder. When I nodded, he handed me a thick envelope and they walked away without another word. My heart dropped to my knees before I even closed the door. I remembered the last time I'd gotten an envelope like that.

It was, as I feared, a restraining order that said that I could not have any contact with my two older children until a hearing in early October. On the first page, the judge's justification spelled out the story Paul had told him, a kernel of truth embellished by a small novella's worth of fiction: I endangered my sons by taking them to live in a shack with no running water; I fed them only soybeans; they dressed in torn, soiled clothing; they'd been exposed to people of low moral character; there were drugs, and orgies. On and On. Sick to my stomach, I read no further, collapsing into myself like one of those folding tin cups my mother used to send to camp. The truth would have been bad enough, I thought. Why the lies? The sensationalism?

My belly felt like a grenade had gone off in it, shards of fear shredding my insides like shrapnel. There was no daddy to bail me out this time. I had no money and no support system. My friends were far away, and my mother was going to eat me alive. Dear God, what would I do? Life without my kids? Unthinkable, unimaginable, impossible.

How would I ever pay a lawyer? How would I even find one? I was a freak, a hippie chick, with hairy legs, long skirts and no bra. I had no home. Except for what I looked like, what would people know of me or my world, other than what they'd seen in TV movies and sensational headlines? Paul wore three-piece suits and worked in a bank and had a house in the suburbs.

This was my fault, running back and forth, leaving us homeless and vulnerable. I knew the boys were always safe, taken care of, fed and loved, surrounded by kind, decent people. But would anyone else see it that way?

September slogged along in a teary blur. I was grateful for my baby. Paralyzed with fear and anguish, I only roused myself to take care of him. I didn't know how many days the hearing would last, so I had to wean him from the breastfeeding I enjoyed so much, the quiet connection that transitions mother and baby into separateness. He did this easily, as if he understood the necessity. We spent hours walking, Jason high on my back in his carrier, through the golden autumn days. The waning warmth of the sun fell gently on my shoulders, the slight tang in the air smelling of Halloween and costumes and too much candy. Of children. The small stone houses sat back from the leafy sidewalks with their bicycle-strewn lawns, whispering from behind their doors of families and home and belonging.

Jason, almost a year old, was just taking his first steps. He was my only sunshine, as my father used to sing to me. "You are my sunshine, my only sunshine, you make me happy when skies are grey..." How daddy loved to sing, even though he couldn't carry a tune to save his life. And he was absolutely loyal, something my mother definitely was not. I missed that safety, knowing there was someone in the world who would always look out for me, even if I did screw up. If only he'd been there then.

I didn't sleep, longing for my boys to be safely asleep in the next room. What were they thinking? Were they scared? Did they miss me? Did someone read them stories before bed and tuck them in? Was anyone making sure that Robert didn't feel alone and David didn't overburden himself with responsibility? Nightmares of Robert crying for me haunted the darkness.

Chapter 23

Men In Dark Suits

I frequently crossed paths with my mother's next-door neighbor, a sweet woman named Rachel, and we often stopped to chat. She was a tall, slim, heavily made-up blond, married to a man much older than she. She loved children and would have loved one of her own, she confided in me, but he didn't. I hated that she'd resigned herself to giving up something she wanted so much. I hated that she painted her lovely face to please a man who didn't seem to care about her very much. I'd met him and I had to bite my tongue. Hard.

Rachel was always happy to see Jason. She'd invite him in and play with him while we talked. After I got the restraining order, she noticed how distraught I was and gently asked what was wrong. I'd had no one to talk to and the story exploded from me like I'd been shaken too long and suddenly popped open. She said she knew a lawyer I could call. Surprisingly, my mother, furious at both me and Paul, had offered money for one. Whatever her motivation, I was grateful, although it was another helping of guilt to take money from her.

One week before my thirty-first birthday, I walked into the darkly paneled law office, my feet sinking softly into the thick carpet. Cool and solemn in his expensive suit, the middle-aged attorney listened to my story quietly, twirling a pencil between two fingers and occasionally scribbling on his yellow legal pad. He looked over the restraining order and without a word reached for the intercom, calling another, younger man into his office. This man, president of the Philadelphia Folksong Society, would handle my case, the older man told me. "He'll understand a case like yours," was how he put it.

Not quite grasping the connection between folk music and custody, other than, in this case, their association with hippies, I nevertheless asked nothing. What would I ask? I had no idea how to fight this battle. My blood seemed to be flowing too slowly, my insides sticky with its thickness. Sick with apprehension, I answered his questions and listened to explanations of legal issues as incomprehensible as twelfth-grade calculus. All I knew was that we were talking about my children, and they weren't with me. They'd been with me since before their first breaths. They were everything, my heart, my purpose; I loved them beyond words. "Please," I begged, "bring my children back to me."

This man's skepticism was obvious. "Maybe saying as little as possible is the best approach," he said. Maybe? He didn't know? "I'll be in touch."

I nodded mutely, at a complete loss.

By the time the hearing began, I hadn't seen or talked to my children in almost two months. I was beside myself with longing, fear and worry. What could they be thinking? Wearing new clothes... a short, denim skirt and flowered blouse... with my legs freshly shaven and my unruly curls pulled tightly into a ponytail, I crept up the stone courthouse steps, my head tucked down into my chest. I was terrified. The sky was a vast slab of granite pressing down upon me.

The first day was brutal. Paul's lawyer described a life bearing very little semblance to the one I'd been living, a life more closely resembling a TV crime drama, the kind where they show dirty, drugged-out women whose children ran wild and unfed and were justifiably taken from them by a kindly young social worker. They couldn't be talking about me! And what could they know about West Virginia and our life there? Or New Mexico or Tennessee? Damn Charles Manson and his lunatic gang, who'd darkened the image of all us longhairs. Damn all those men who knew nothing of a mother's heart.

The second day, Barb, who had been subpoenaed and come down from Vermont, sat on the witness stand, her back straight and her long, dark skirt wrapped tightly around her calves. Although I knew she was coming, it was still painful to see her there, under fire because of me. Paul's lawyer pounded her about our relationship and life in West Virginia. Where did we sleep and where did the children sleep? How about Nick? What was the relationship between the three of us? (How did he know about Nick?) What did we eat? Was the milk we drank pasteurized? How did we bathe and wash clothes?

Barb's responses were angry and emphatic. When he asked what drugs we used, she lost her cool and practically screamed at him, "There were no drugs. You're making all this up!" And that was true. There was a vast difference between the sex-drugs-and-rock-and-roll hippies and real peace-love-and-understanding flower children. I'd played around with pot after the divorce, but I hadn't been aware of any drugs anywhere we'd been. They weren't necessary. We were on a natural high. It sounds hokey, but it was true.

Then Paul's lawyer brought out pictures that were taken with David's little Kodak Instamatic. In the six months Barb stayed with us, David became interested in the photography she was doing. It was her major at Goddard. She even set up a darkroom in one of the bathrooms.

I still remember him busily clicking away everywhere we went. I gave it no thought when he took the camera to his father's.

The pictures were damning, at least to some eyes, because in many of them we wore no clothes. It was hot in West Virginia; we often went naked. It was as natural in that setting as breathing. But in this courtroom, on this day, it just seemed ugly. Dirty. Even to me. Had I been wrong to think it was okay? Or was my mistake underestimating, ignoring really, the threat to someone like me from the straight world? Now I knew what it felt like to come up against the system as a "minority." I'd never thought about it. Was it arrogance? Naivety? I forgot to be cautious, forgot that I needed to be. And left my babies right in the middle.

"What were all of you doing out there together... naked?" John's lawyer asked Barb, his insinuating tone oozing across the large room like a wave of dirty motor oil. "In front of the children," he added emphatically.

"It was hot. We weren't *doing* anything." Barb was tight-lipped.

The pictures were the only actual evidence that was presented. Two other people were called to testify: David's third grade teacher, whose praise for David and for me warmed my frozen heart; and a former neighbor who apologized to me as she walked to the witness stand to disclose her awareness of my use of marijuana, which I'd only recently discovered and foolishly discussed with her.

Paul accused me of having affairs with men who didn't exist and orgies on the lawn where the children could see, of exposing them to drugs and "those freaks," whom he described as somewhere between debauched and demonic. He righteously claimed that Barb and I had a homosexual relationship, while he'd just finished listing all my fictional male lovers. "She goes both ways," he explained primly when the judge questioned him on this.

I was stunned. Not in the furthest reaches of my imagination would I have foreseen this. To hear all the kind and decent people I'd met everywhere we went demeaned like that made my body ache like an emotional flu. I wanted to hide in my bed and sip chamomile tea until I woke up to find this was all just a terrible nightmare.

What kind of mind dreamed up stuff like this? Was it the lawyer and his win-at-any-cost mentality or was it my ex-husband, who feared anything outside his personal norm? Had I been married to a man with such a warped mentality? How could anyone believe this? But I was looking from the inside out, from *my* personal norms and I was ridiculously naive.

Overwhelmed and defeated at the end of the first two days, I returned to Jason, who was with Rachel. Paul's attorney had made sure we were heard by the most conservative judge in the county. My lawyer seemed to say very little and asked few questions. I wanted him to fight, to knock down every single lie Paul told, poke holes in every argument and rip this whole act to pieces. Wasn't that what he should have been doing?

What did I know of the world really, beyond three meals a day, and sorting small clothing, stories of misfit dogs and mice with tiny furniture who snuggled in front of cozy wee fireplaces? What did I know of courtrooms and legal maneuvering and how helpless a poor, single mother can be against men in dark suits?

On the third day, David and Robert were brought in to speak to the judge. Their hair was cut short and they wore small, button-down shirts and pressed khakis. It seemed like forever since I'd seen them. Robert carried a huge toy truck under each arm. When they saw me, they both looked down and said nothing. When I moved to greet them, they looked to their father for permission. Rob inched closer to David, who stiffly mumbled hi. I just knew if I reached to touch them, they would flinch. I could not bear it. I couldn't. My heart felt like someone had cut open my chest and punched it down, like yeast risen bread. It was hard to breathe.

According to my lawyer the kids told the judge they'd be okay living with either one of us. Years later, however, David confessed that Paul told them I'd agreed it was best for them to stay with him. "We thought you didn't want us anymore," he explained.

In his summation, my lawyer finally said the things I'd been hoping to hear, defending my character, my choices and my devotion to my kids. He suggested that although the judge might not understand or approve of the life I'd lived, that life was not necessarily the way it had been described. It was not necessarily immoral or objectionable, just different. He recalled the testimony of David's teacher, who came to court for us voluntarily and spoke so highly of David and me, of how impressed he'd been with the kind of boy David was, and with what he'd observed as my parenting style. A small glimmer of hope fluttered through me like a lost butterfly.

And then, thankfully, it was over. There was nothing left to do but wait for the judge's decision. Immediately I went out and bought a half dozen pairs of white cotton underpants. Knowing that Paul's seamy description of my life reflected the view through his own dirty lens and not the truth of my experience didn't prevent me from feeling soiled. White cotton, however, did not make me feel any cleaner. I may not have been guilty of the things I'd been accused of, but ultimately, like Lady Macbeth, the damn spot of responsibility remained on my hands.

A short time later I received a letter from Linda and learned that Paul had hired a private investigator and sent him to West Virginia. "Who is this guy and what did he want here?" she wrote. "He asked all sorts of strange questions about you and Barb and where we get milk and how many people live in our house. He kept trying to get us to say things that just aren't true. What's going on?"

I knew that nothing either Bob or Linda said could have fed this fire. Paul and his lawyer had painted an ugly picture of my life. Would the judge give such a blazingly overdramatic story any credence? Was there any chance at all that he'd see through it? I wasn't hopeful. I shrank further and further into myself each day, wishing only to disappear from where I was and magically turn up in the safe, gentle world of "those hippies" Paul sneered at so maliciously.

I made a half-hearted attempt to look for an apartment, calling several and then not going to see them. If the children didn't come back and there was no child support, I wouldn't be able to afford my own place. School had started and David and Robert were attending the elementary near Paul. I didn't want to put them through another change, so I'd want to stay nearby. Should I look for a job? What skills did I have? Who would watch Jason? Nothing was clear... not what to do, where to live, or how to survive. I had no faith in my ability to make sensible decisions and was barely rational. My head was a snake pit, my heart a throbbing wound.

The decision came down in mid-November. My boys were not coming back to me. I was allowed to see them on alternate weekends, only in the presence of my mother, who, as much as she'd seemed to dislike Paul through the years, apparently disliked me more, and had bad-mouthed me enough that he'd called her as a witness against me. (To her credit, she refused.)

My days were focused on taking care of Jason and little else. We read the simple stories toddlers love, especially his favorite, *Corduroy*, about a lonely stuffed bear who sat on a shelf in the store because no one wanted him. That book remained a favorite for years and it saddened me to realize what he must have felt.

We went to the playground regularly, where I strapped him on the swings and pushed as hard as I could, finding some solace in his happy giggles. Every day we walked through the neighborhood streets watching the seasons change... first the gold and orange leaves piling up by the curb, the bright colors gradually fading into the drab hues of winter. Then we trudged through the innocent white of newly-fallen snow, too soon tarnished by the world. Walking was one of the few things that soothed me. When we were indoors, I sat by the sliding glass doors to the small balcony in a warm patch of sunlight, endless tears pouring down my cheeks while Jason played with his toys, trying to fit the different shaped wood blocks into the appropriate holes. Something I seemed unable to do with my life.

I had nothing. My mother bought us food and clothes for Jason. Other than that, I had only a small amount of money left from my father. I knew I needed help, but fear of someone deciding I was actually insane, or unfit, and taking Jason away from me too, kept me from seeking it. I was not even close to rational.

Phyllis Redman

Chapter 24

When The Devil Laughed

The months slid by in a fog. My thinking was cloudy, circuitous, my thoughts wandering aimlessly, going nowhere. I hid behind the bare, daily necessities of meals and laundry, playground trips and walks with Jason. I couldn't get a job, I told myself, because my baby needed me there, but really the thought of going out into the world was incomprehensible. Ordinary conversation was beyond me. How would I answer a simple "How are you?"

Jason's birthday, barely noticed during the hearing, was only quietly acknowledged a year later. I saw David and Robert on my allotted weekends, when I attempted to create some fun... a trip to the zoo, a movie, a train ride into center city. But even I knew it wasn't much fun at all. We were so sadly uncomfortable with each other. None of us knew how to do this. I didn't feel like a mother, or even an adult. I got accustomed to celebrating birthdays and holidays after they'd passed. None of it was the least bit festive; I was keenly aware of all I didn't have to offer.

My mother was clearly the authority figure, one who didn't hesitate to criticize and embarrass me every chance she got, frequently commenting to her grandchildren about what a mess their mother was. Like an abused dog, I cringed and receded further into myself each time she opened her mouth. How could I respond, when I was living in her home and completely dependent, without any money and unable to see my kids without her?

I couldn't sleep. Longing for my boys to be nestled safely in the next room, I lay awake for hours, or paced the small living room all night, wondering if they were okay. Did they miss me?

Did someone sing them "Big Rock Candy Mountain" before they left the room, as I had every night for years? Robert was so young. Nightmares where I felt him crying for me haunted the darkness. When the weekend came, David would often tell me that yes, Rob did cry for me in the night. They were not nightmares at all, but a mother's finely tuned senses, still palpable, like the phantom pain of the amputee whose long gone limbs continue to throb through the night.

Robert was traumatized and got sick over and over, running fevers, coughing, complaining of upset stomachs. Willing, as always, to see only what he chose to, Paul took him to several doctors and eventually down to Children's Hospital in Philadelphia to be evaluated. At one point, Rob was so overmedicated he could barely speak. His hands shook. I was frantic and called the doctor at CHOP who told me flat out that he believed Rob's condition to be psychosomatic, that his father would not consider that possibility, and therefore there was nothing he could do other than prescribe medication. As the non-custodial parent, I had no rights. I called my lawyer. "You'll never prove it," he said with finality. I couldn't bear the helplessness.

A year later, unable to afford needed repairs on the VW bus, I reluctantly sold it. I needed to get a job, but not only did I have no marketable skills, I now had no transportation either. Nor was I yet in any state of mind to go out into the world and function like a normal human being.

I knew I needed help; I had no support system whatsoever. My friends were all out west and had no idea what to do for me. My sister and brother ignored me. I'd hear my mother on the phone with her sisters, telling them how crazy I was, such a mess, she didn't know what to do with me. Each word burned into my soul, my own scarlet letters of shame. Steeped in shame and grief, pieces of my broken heart seeped into every cell of my being like ink dripped slowly into water, I was so completely undone, so totally irrational, that in my dreams the devil was laughing at me. "I have your children," he cackled. I'd wake up sobbing into my pillow, not wanting my mother to hear me and think she was right, although I wondered if she really was.

For a long time I failed to see the effects on Jason of having no one in his life except a grieving mother and a hysterical grandmother shrieking day and night about what the neighbors thought. Among other things. My mother was unable to come to terms with her privacy being torn away by the presence of her frizzy-haired, unshaven daughter and her illegitimate son, there for all the world to see. Nor with the disarray of her decor. Puzzles and Fisher Price trucks were strewn across her white carpet, Jason's little feet were on her white love seats. She needed the anonymity of privacy and the outward order of a stylishly decorated home as buffers between her and a world she didn't really know how to navigate. Appearances were her only protection. I took that from her.

Jason turned three and then four, his formative years shaped by this monumental dysfunction. I overcompensated by rarely saying no, pouring his milk rather than letting him do it himself so I wouldn't bring on a sharp "Do it for him! I don't want milk on everything," or a round of slamming cabinets. I did it so I might possibly retain some semblance of parental authority, sham though it was. I did it to ward off further humiliation and shaming.

At night Jason wouldn't go to sleep without me beside him. He learned the game quickly - make some noise and he'd get what he wanted. This was neither to his benefit nor mine and nothing like I raised his brothers.

I did it to make up for all I didn't have to give him.

Cindy wrote from New Mexico often, pleading with me to bring Jason and make a new life out there. Even Mike, after years of silence, wrote and asked me to join him in California. I was surprised. I wanted to go to him and start over. I knew the life I was living couldn't possibly be the best thing for Jason. But how could I leave David and Robert? I didn't know if being there really did them any good, but I simply couldn't bear the thought of not seeing them. Nor was I willing to risk them thinking their mother didn't care enough to stay near them. At the time I didn't foresee that I would be at my mother's until Jason was eight years old.

Phyllis Redman

Chapter 25

Stepping Ashore

On one of our walks in the spring of 1978, I rediscovered a small yarn shop down a side street behind the stores that lined York Road in Jenkintown. I'd bought yarns there for years before I went away. Pushing Jason's stroller through the wide front door, I found myself surrounded by shelves and cubbyholes packed with skeins of brightly colored yarns of every weight, texture and fiber imaginable. Soft white angoras, nubby orange cottons, green and blue variegated wools, red chenille. For the first time in years a surge of interest ran through me. Every Christmas I used to make the kids sweaters and hats, but I'd made nothing since returning to the area. The click of the needles, the gradual appearance of fabric, the hypnotic movement of my hands completely absorbed my attention and had always soothed me.

Browsing through the magazines piled high on a shelf, I found a set of patterns for little dolls, each dressed in a traditional outfit from a different country, and a book with colorful, happy designs for children's sweaters. I bought enough of a heathery, emerald green yarn for a pullover for Jason, and small amounts of a dozen colors for the dolls and left the shop with an unaccustomed tickle of excitement in my belly to have a project to work on.

I started immediately, making a small sample doll for practice, with a tiny sweater from the green yarn for Jason and a pair of red pants. Much to my surprise, Jason held onto that doll for dear life, clutching it in his small hands and holding it close when he went to sleep. Although he saw his brothers twice a month, they were years older than he and had a closeness from which he was excluded. They weren't unkind, but they'd had each other for years and their younger brother wasn't part of their everyday lives. Jason was a lonely little boy.

That summer during afternoons at the apartment house's pool, with my needles clicking together softly, I watched Jason splash in the baby pool by my feet. One day I looked up to see a short, orange-haired woman standing beside me, watching my hands closely. I'd seen her before, but we'd never spoken.

"What are you making?" she asked curiously. I was using double-pointed needles which are tricky to work with. That doll, the third in the set, was the Japanese one, dressed in a kimono, complete with obi and sandals. "That looks difficult."

"Are you a knitter?" I asked.

She nodded and sat down in the chair beside me. "You're Sylvia Redman's daughter, aren't you? I'm Edie Brown. On the sixth floor."

I smiled. "Yeah, I'm Sylvia's wayward kid. And that's Jason." I pointed to my three-year-old.

Edie smiled back. "Oh we know all about you. So, what are you making?"

"A doll. One of a set."

"You must be good. That looks complicated. I've only made sweaters. Baby sweaters."

"It's not simple, but it's lots of fun. There's a whole set, each from a different country. Making these is keeping me sane."

"Do you think you could help me put a sweater together? I can make the pieces okay, but the finishing is sloppy. Ruins the whole thing. I'd pay you."

"Sure. I like the finishing work. Bring it down," I replied with surprise.

Soon other women were showing me their baby blankets and cardigans, and the complicated patterns they found daunting. They knocked on my mother's door as if it were actually my home. Could I sew the pieces of their latest sweater together for them, or crochet an edge around the carriage blanket for their grandson? They'd pay me too of course. I was good at finishing and enjoyed it, enjoyed taking all those different pieces and making them into something you could wear or cover someone with. But my mother was not happy with these intrusions into what she considered her shameful existence. Meaning me.

Gradually I became comfortable again with human contact. That I was not a pariah to those women was surprising and reassuring. I shaved my legs and tied my wild hair back. I was tired of being stared at. I wanted to be part of something, even the somewhat uncomfortable society of Beaver Hill Apartments, where the great majority of the residents were twenty or more years older than I, wealthy, and everything I'd wanted so much to escape.

In time Jason and I became known to many of the residents. I had a small business going, which didn't bring in a lot of money, but did somewhat normalize my life. And restore a modicum of self-confidence. It was good for Jason to have people who talked to him, unlike his grandmother, who'd never spoken much to her own children, and his mother, who was only now beginning to recover some sense of normalcy. Those were my first steps ashore onto the land of the living.

Chapter 26

Five Years Later

At the pool one hot Sunday afternoon midway through the summer of 1983, as I relaxed under an umbrella at the pool doing the New York Times crossword, I met Kurt. Weekends were treasured that year. I'd started working as a customer service representative at Prudential AARP, advising seniors around the country about Medicare supplemental policies. After going on welfare to get enough money for a car, an old, butter yellow Datsun station wagon, the employment office found me the job. For the first time since David was born, I stepped out into the world of full-time working adults. The puzzle was my reward after a tiring week.

The pool was Jason and my sanctuary during the summer, a place where we both escaped the pressures and loneliness of our lives. The previous summer, two young lifeguards befriended Jason and taught him to swim and he loved it more than anything I'd ever seen him do. He was shy and hadn't made many friends at school, but several children lived at Beaver Hill by then, and sometimes, as that day, he had other children to play with. Some small measure of tranquility settled over me, fluttering lightly in my belly like a butterfly in unfamiliar territory. Allowing myself this taste of peace was a struggle. "I don't deserve it" was woven into the fabric of everything I was.

Kurt sat down in the chair next to mine. "Okay, I'm impressed. Couldn't do one of those," he nodded toward the newspaper in my hand, "if I were facing a firing squad."

I looked up and smiled. He was a handsome man, with an interesting little scar across the side of his cheek, just under his right eye. He was dark and enticing like a pirate from an old Errol Flynn movie. "It's my treat of the week. You get a feel for them after a while," I said, as I put the paper down.

It had been almost nine years since I'd connected with any man, or even wanted to. Although not yet forty, my libido had been dormant for a long time, a vaguely remembered life force withering in the darkness of my misery. I was surprised, and a little relieved, to feel it surface.

"So what are you doing in the land of senior living?" he asked.

"Long story. Wrecked my life, trying to rebuild." My belly contracted in response to my words. "Do you live here or are you visiting your parents?"

He looked at me for a moment. "Well, we have something in common already. Wrecked my life, here to rebuild." His voice was rueful.

"What did you do?"

"Gambling. Lost it all... the wife, the house, the business." He frowned and shook his head. "Stupid. What about you?"

Where to start. "Like I said, long story. Traveled too long, my ex took me to court and got custody of my two older kids - that's my youngest there in the orange trunks - and I fell apart. For a long time. I'm just getting going again, seven long years later."

Both lonely and wounded, we connected quickly, the hippie and the material man. Yet, odd couple that we were, we laughed together and gave each other some much needed companionship. He was interested in where I'd been and who I was. I was intrigued by his interest. He wanted to know what kind of person wanted to change the world. He said that had never been his focal point. He was tough and cold, although not to me. He was nothing like the people I held dear.

"What do you see in a man like me?" he asked one night, his hand warm on my shoulder. "You're kind and concerned about the world. I don't really give a damn."

I didn't tell him how moved I was by his honest and very accurate assessment of himself. I was touched that he saw something he deemed "better" and wanted it. I just smiled and moved closer to him on the couch. Perhaps I should have told him what I thought, I don't know. He was strong and attentive, and for the first time in ages, someone was there for me.

We continued to see each other, and after two years rented a small house nearby. Kurt's daughter, Carol, who was three months younger than Jason, was going to come live with us. She was a difficult child, tough like her father, argumentative and headstrong. Her mother threw in the towel. "If you want her," she told Kurt, "she's all yours."

Kurt thought it would be good for his daughter. "She needs someone patient and gentle," he said. I thought it would be a good thing because Kurt was not as attentive to Jason as I would have liked, and I hoped his parenting instincts would kick in with his daughter there. And that Carol and Jason might form some kind of friendship. We could be a family. None of those things happened.

Unfortunately, healthy relationships do not grow out of choices made by emotionally unhealthy people. There was much I liked about Kurt, but I didn't love him. He appreciated me but didn't love me either. Not once had we used that word. Not once had we melted together in surrender to some overwhelming passion. Often we had nothing to say to each other at all. Something fundamental was missing.

One night, after returning with the kids from the ice cream shop down the street, Kurt made a confession. "There was a man there with three kids, three little boys just hanging on him," he said. Seated at the kitchen table across from me, he shook his head ruefully. "I envied that man, happy to have those rug rats climbing all over him. The little one was on his shoulders, another wrapped around his legs and the oldest clinging to his hand. I'd like to be that way, comfortable with all that touchy-feely stuff. But I'm not. I'm just not."

Accurate once again. He wasn't, and that other man was the one I wanted for Jason. Someone who would hug him, throw a ball around with him on the front lawn, or share a real conversation. Someone who'd act like a dad.

Nor did Jason and Carol get along. She was disdainful and impatient with his insecurity and social clumsiness. He'd had only limited experience with relationships of any kind, other than a building full of grandmothers indulging him, like I did. He balked at doing homework, slamming his notebook down on the kitchen table. He refused to do chores, or most anything he was asked to do. He had temper tantrums, slamming doors and cabinets as his grandmother had. The impact of my depression, and the life it had created for so much of his, was clearly visible.

"Don't be such a baby," Carol snapped haughtily when Jason got frustrated with homework or argued about bedtime. "Just do it." I tried to mediate, but Kurt stayed out of it. Without his involvement, how could we possibly be a family? And I needed help.

Jason didn't have Carol's maturity or discipline. He had not had anything one would call a normal childhood. He had no idea what it felt like to have a father or to be part of anything and had never witnessed cooperation or supportiveness between people. Kurt did nothing to change that. He showed no desire to be a parent, or a friend, to my boy at all. In fact, he wasn't the most devoted parent to his own child.

Kurt and I gave each other a hand to hold in order to move on. I was grateful for the good we'd shared. We had some sweetness, some fun, and forward momentum for our lives. I was out of my mother's at last! But when our two-year lease was up, he found an apartment for himself and Carol and we said goodbye. I was scared and sad, but not heartbroken.

Jason, however, took it harder than I expected. He moped around, said little and stayed in his room most of the time. Surprised, I realized that Kurt was the closest he'd ever come to having a father, and no matter how little Kurt had given, for Jason this was a real loss.

Chapter 27

On My Own

Jason was about to enter seventh grade when we moved into our own place for the first time since he was an infant. Elkins Park Gardens was a u-shaped complex wedged between a gothic, three-story stone building that was once Cheltenham High School and a small park with a playground, tennis courts and a track where I could see people jogging any time of the day. Tookany Creek ran down the middle of the 'u,' visible from the back windows of our two-bedroom apartment. Though we were minutes from where I grew up, the trees out front and the creek brought back some of the connection with nature I'd grown to love.

I gave Jason the master bedroom so he could have his own boy world, with space for a desk, his fish tank and, hopefully, friends to hang out with. We were fortunate to find a place that allowed Jason's beloved Yoyo, the little black mutt we adopted while living with Kurt. I was grateful to that sweet dog who gave Jason so much love.

Happy to be in our own space, Jason and I had fun going to yard sales and flea markets, buying pictures, small tables and knickknacks to create a homey space. My mother donated lamps, kitchen stuff and a bed, and bought us a sectional sofa, more to her taste than mine with its quiet beige tones, but I was grateful, nonetheless. Surprisingly, she'd become supportive and interested in my life, now that I was no longer an embarrassment to her. She never did like Kurt and stayed away the two years I was with him. Now she was suddenly a mother with a child who needed the kind of help she was comfortable giving.

However, Jason was still distraught over the breakup of the only family he'd ever known. He hated going to school and was willing to get on the bus only because I told him the authorities would come after me if he didn't. He was seriously depressed, reluctant to get out of bed in the morning and moping in his room in the afternoons. The school put him on suicide watch, recommended therapy and gave me the name of someone to see. After a half dozen sessions, Jason said, "He doesn't say anything you haven't already said, mom," and we stopped going. I didn't know what to do for him.

I was split between the pleasure of being on my own and fear for my son. I was lonely too. I longed for the world I'd left behind years before, where every child, and adult, mattered to the community. Where no one was left to feel invisible and alone.

I had no close friends. My brother had cut himself off from all of us. My sister lived in New York and we rarely communicated. Neither had ever really been part of my life nor shown any interest in my kids. I'd stopped hoping for that a long time before then. I'd made some effort, especially with my brother, inviting him along to concerts and events back in the days before I went out west, but he'd rarely reciprocated, inviting Jason and me to Thanksgiving only twice in all the years I was with my mother. Although he had a daughter near Jason's age, family connections simply didn't exist for us.

I continued through the years to see David and Robert every other weekend, but I never felt a part of their lives. At first I tried to stay connected. I went to their school to see how they were doing, where they told me they couldn't speak to me because I was not the custodial parent. I had the distinct feeling they'd been warned about me.

I was not invited to their Bar Mitzvahs... at least not by Paul. The boys themselves asked me to come, which I did. To the services only, not the parties afterward.

One rainy day I was shopping near their school and happened to see Robert. It was raining and I offered him a ride home. He got in trouble, he told me later, for getting in the car with me. Was Paul having me watched? How had he known? I felt like a criminal and the kids only ended up feeling uncomfortable. I finally gave up.

One day during the first spring season in our new home, I ran into an old friend from high school, who was back in the area visiting her parents. She lived in Virginia, where she taught secondary English and language arts.

"This is what you should be doing, Phyllis," she told me, nodding her head emphatically and actually waving a polished pink fingernail before my nose. "English was always your favorite class. You'd love teaching."

My job as a customer service rep had become boring and didn't pay enough. Teaching was what my father had wanted me to do, but it never appealed to me. I hated telling people what to do, was not very good at it, and, in fact, was probably the world's worst disciplinarian. I really wanted to be some kind of therapist, always had, but I knew I had neither the drive, patience, time nor money for that much schooling. A teaching certificate, on the other hand, could get me a living wage with only a bachelor's degree.

Could I do it, I wondered? Did I want to go back to school, sit in classrooms and listen to lectures? Write papers? I had no great desire to be a teacher and couldn't imagine where the money would come from for school fees and living expenses. Having given up the idea of an alternative lifestyle, despite the stubborn longing that just wouldn't go away, it was clear I wasn't going anywhere. Not without David and Robert. Like a worn toy top, I'd spun myself out and tipped over for the last time. There was nothing left to do but take it from where I was. How ironic that when I finally landed, it was literally right back where I started. But at that moment, all I wanted was to be an independent, functioning adult who could create some happiness for my youngest son. I wanted to own my life.

My mother was all the family Jason and I had and was displaying hitherto unseen concern for our wellbeing. "If you want to go back to school and complete your degree, Phyl, I'll pay your rent. You never should have quit when David was born anyway," she said when I called to discuss the idea. "It's what you should have done a long time ago."

Was this the same mom who was willing to swear on paper her refusal to help me financially when I went on welfare so I could buy a car, even though she was quite well-off? Was I finally getting it right? Feeling much like the little girl who once stood on the edge of the swimming pool, reluctantly contemplating my face slamming into the cold water, I began the process of applying for Pell grants, registering for admission and choosing courses at Temple University in Philadelphia. Boy, you really never know where life is going to take you.

At the same time, I got a part-time job in the after-school daycare program at Wyncote Elementary, just a few minutes from home. It was only a small, supplemental income, but I needed it. And enjoyed it. I liked being around little kids again, and my co-teacher, Christine, was fun to work with. I loved hearing the giggles, and "Miss Phyllis, Miss Phyllis" from across the playground, the feel of small hands slipped trustingly into mine once again. It had been a long time since I'd experienced the ease of relating to young children, where a kiss on the palm of a small, grubby hand is enough to set the whole world right. That I knew how to do.

Chapter 28

Back To School

Two years after moving into the apartment I was a student again. Temple University is in North Philadelphia, in the heart of the ghetto. Driving to classes was unpleasant, getting a parking place near campus problematic, the walk there hurried and uneasy. Broken bottles, beer cans, cigarette butts, squashed coffee cups and soda cans lined the curbs like perverted necklaces draped around the throats of the dirty, rundown houses above them. Many were abandoned, gazing down vacantly through the jagged glass of their gouged out eyes. Every time I made it to Mitten Hall safely was a small victory.

Once on campus though, I was eighteen again, a young girl looking to the future that loomed ahead, as it had so long ago, full of promise and possibility. I had two-plus years of credits that had transferred from Miami University in Ohio, most of which were accepted to fill elective requirements. However, I still had to take all the courses needed for a degree in secondary education, so I had at least two years of schooling ahead of me before I would be certified.

Being older than the average student, I discovered, was an asset. Despite my doubts, being back in the classroom offered a more pleasing perspective on myself than I'd had in a long time. I'd gathered some wisdom and knowledge about life along the way. A piece of myself that was lost during the hearing and the years at my mother's started coming back to life. I began to feel like who I really was.

My teachers loved me. My work ethic was, in their eyes, remarkable. As was my memory when we discussed world events and leaders. My avid interest in politics, going back to high school, paid off in the halls of academia. I knew who Ramsey Clark was! My knitting business, my job at Prudential/AARP, my travels and life experience all came together now to form a picture of myself that was, inch by inch, becoming one I could make some small measure of peace with.

Jason was in high school then, and although there was a lot of damage to be mended, he was surviving and had some friends. After many phone calls and visits to the school, I finally connected with someone to mentor my son, a gym teacher with a real interest in his students and an easy way with Jason, who responded to the attention like the lonely child he'd always been. I could breathe a little easier.

Tomorrow was becoming a place of possibility... a light at the end of the long tunnel of despair through which I'd been inching for a long, long time. I was tired of the darkness of failure and the cold stranglehold of shame. I was on my way, working hard, and I could feel the warmth of that light. Just as on a rainy spring evening twenty years before, I stood, nervous and excited, at the threshold of an unknown future. What would it look like when I got there?

Phyllis Redman

Epilogue

I graduated from Temple University in 1991 and taught in the Philadelphia School District until I retired in 2008. I grew up there. You'd better be an adult in an inner-city classroom! I had to be in charge... and after a while I was. And my students liked it that way. I was real with those kids and they appreciated that too. I thank them for all the lessons they taught me.

After yet another unhappy relationship, I found a teacher named David Michael, with whom I began the healing work I'd needed to do for years. He guided me, with kindness, wisdom and humor, through those first steps to becoming a healthy, whole adult, and led me to Woman Within International, an organization of strong, compassionate and wise women supporting each other in their personal healing and growth. For the last twenty years I've sat in a circle of women who have become my family, my sisters, my bedrock through every up, down and sideways turn in life. It is their steady and unflinching support and love that has enabled me to find my voice and stand up in the world and use it. Sandy Freid, Cindee Levow, Verna Tweddale, Jacquie Price, Susan Odhner, Jeanne Farr, Shan Holt, Tina Silverman and Hollis Payer, thank you.

In 2008, shortly after I retired, I reconnected with an old friend from high school, the world I tried to leave behind. We just celebrated our ten-year anniversary. Harry and I work hard to have a healthy, honest, loving relationship. We share it all... laughter, tears, children and grandchildren. We are family. It took most of a lifetime.

My sons are married now, with children of their own. Our relations are warm and close. The sorrow of losing so much of their early years, for the lasting impact I see in Jason, is not gone, but neither does it run my life anymore. Part of the fabric of my being, it lives more or less at peace with all the other facets of a life experience. David, Robert, Jason...you are my deepest and most abiding loves. This is, above all, a love letter to the three of you. It was all always for you.

Author's Notes and Acknowledgments

All the cliches about short term memory being the first to go are holding up in my mid- seventies. Although I'm often hazy about yesterday, my memory of the period of my life covered in these pages is surprisingly sharp. I can see the sky above the Texas Panhandle, and the Plaza in Santa Fe as clearly as I did that morning in 1974. The beauty of our arrival in Vermont, after a record-breaking blizzard, is forever etched into my memory, as is the quiet comfort of the forest in Tennessee and the hollows of West Virginia.

I also remember conversations with great clarity, although I have taken a fair degree of poetic license in resurrecting them. Still, the meaning is accurate.

Paul and I have made some degree of peace. We were very young and it's been a long time.

I have changed some names and been true to others, to honor those who carry them. Barb is Barbara DeMarco-Barrett, who has inspired me more than she has any idea, with her make-things-happen spirit and her wonderful writing. David Michael, my teacher and friend, changed my life forever. Sandy Freid's honesty and attention always make me a better person. And Cindy Greene, who left this earthly plane much too young. Thank you Cindy, for traveling across a continent to keep me company because you loved me.

A special thanks to Edie Weinstein, editor and friend, who is a walking inspiration in so many ways.

And to Kathy Sheeder Bonanno, without whom this story would not have been written, whose wisdom, patience, skill and humor carried me through it all. I love you, I miss you, and I'm pissed as hell that you're no longer here.

About the Author

Phyllis Redman is a retired high school English teacher and current tutor, who works mainly with young people with learning issues. Phyllis is, and has been, a political activist and spiritual seeker and a member of Woman Within International, an organization where women support each other in their personal growth and struggles, and which she credits with her becoming the woman she is today. She lives outside Philadelphia with her partner, Harry, and has three grown sons and five grandchildren. You can read her blog at: mamatree5@wordpress.com.